VESTED!

VESTED!

THE MILLENNIAL'S GUIDE TO THE NEXT GENERATION OF INVESTING

WILLIAM MCDONALD

NEW DEGREE PRESS

VESTED!

The Millennial's Guide to the Next Generation of Investing

ISBN   978-1-5445-0028-7 *Paperback*

       978-1-5445-0029-4 *Ebook*

To my father, who instilled the entrepreneurial
spirit in me from the very beginning.

CONTENTS

"The best way to predict the future is to create it"

- PETER DRUCKER

.

ABOUT THE AUTHOR

———

William McDonald is the founder of The Vested Investor, an organization focused on educating millennials about the next generation of investment opportunities around alternative investments.

Will's passion for entrepreneurship, innovation and growth-oriented organizations began at an early age. Having grown up around the campaign trail, Will saw firsthand the value that a successful political team could build for a candidate. Moving this interest for value creation to the business world, Will began working for small growth companies while in high school, having founded his first company during his junior year.

Will was incredibility active in entrepreneurial and startup activities at Georgetown University, serving as co-president of Georgetown's entrepreneurial initiative, Startup Hoyas. He also found time to study finance, making alternative investments the perfect passion. An active investor in a variety of alternative investment types, Will thinks "crowd-investing" will transform our economy from the ground up. Will continues to speak, write and advise on the trends of millennial investing in these new asset classes and platforms.

INTRODUCTION

———

Millennials have a unique outlook on life. We are a generation that cares more about the experiences that we have than the tangible goods that we own. One that cares more about finding a way to give back to our community than merely striving for personal gain. And we are more concerned with building a community around us rather than operating individually for our own benefit.

Born in the age of the Internet, we as millennials have grown up in an unprecedented period of connectivity. Having immediate access to information, entertainment, shopping, communications and one another, all in real time and in the palm of our hands has profoundly impacted how we view the world. This millennial mindset of connection has led us to visualize a fundamental shift in how our world operates and how individuals can and should live their lives. As a generation we are paving the way for an entirely new approach to both our society and our economy.

THE NEW SHARING ECONOMY

In the always connected sharing economy of today, we are more comfortable than ever before with sharing not only our life experiences but our personal resources with one another. Instagram and Facebook led the way in sharing life experiences, but this sharing mindset is now expanding into other dimensions of the economy.

While in the past people may have turned to Western Union to exchange money, our generation is using Vemno. We don't look for hotels anymore because we know we can book an AirBnb and rent someone's apartment. And we don't hail cabs, because we can grab an Uber with our phone and get a ride in someone else's car.

We simply do not think about life in the same way that our parents and grandparents did. However in the case of investing, we often feel as if we are left with the same options that have been around for so long. The innovation we have seen transform so many industries seems to be lacking when it comes to our investing world, instead often defaulting to established banks and the stock market.

Just like Uber transformed the taxi industry and AirBnb transformed the hospitality scene, there is a wave of companies and entrepreneurs who are reshaping the investing world as we know it. These innovators are creating a new approach for how people are able to make and receive loans, as well how businesses can secure the money needed to start, grow or expand. These financial innovators are combining the two most powerful and transformative platforms, the Internet and social networks, to radically transform the relatively stodgy world of investing.

It's a revolution, just what you might expect from millennials.

Investing our hard-earned money in the Wall Street casino is no longer the only choice. Rather, innovative investing platforms now enable us to invest our savings directly into real businesses and real people. This new wave of investing is improving peoples lives and helping to create jobs and make a real impact in the economy around us.

With crowd investing we are now able to invest our savings in a personal loan, helping someone to finance their first mortgage and realize the dream of buying their first home. We can invest directly into a small business, enabling them to expand and hire that next employee. We are able to invest in a small team of entrepreneurs setting out to build the next great business. By leveraging the power of social networks and the Internet, we are able to organize as an investing "crowd" to support the next great wave of value creation. At the same time we are taking power away from big banks and other large financial institutions and putting it back in the hands of the people. We are investing our resources in those who may have not been able to get the money they needed from the big banks, and help them to realize their dreams, growing our economy from the inside out.

We are democratizing investing. By taking our own money and reinvesting it in those around us we are building jobs and stimulating economic development.

This revolution is not about individuals buying and selling shares in the public stock market. It is about a different type of investing and a richer set of returns for you as an individual investor. This is about a social return you receive from knowing that not only can you earn money on your investment but that your investment can help support business growth and individual progress from the ground up.

If you had a thousand dollars to invest, would you invest in a random stock on the market or that small business in your hometown, knowing that your returns would be the same?

Should a faceless bank be the one to decide what business opportunities make the most sense, or should it be the people who are potential customers and who believe in the idea and want to support the owner? Investment should come from those who can buy into a vision and offer their financial support to those who have the passion to create value in the economy. Who better to decide if a new store should receive that loan or start-up investment than the members of the local community. The crowdfunding movement creates a direct connection between individuals with money to loan or invest, and credit worthy individuals and small business owners.

Technology is paving the way for how millennials can directly impact the economy and is reshaping how we support the next great wave of value creation. By leveraging the emerging world of crowd investing we can make sure that those who deserve loans receive them. We can ensure that the businesses of tomorrow can be properly funded by those who support and believe in their ideas.

We are at the forefront of an economic revolution that is about to force a ripple effect across our country. This revolution can help individuals realize their personal dreams and help business owners and entrepreneurs create jobs and grow our economy. We can harness this revolution to create lasting value for ourselves and our country.

* * *

Welcome to the next generation of investing.

In an age when sharing is paramount, millennials can stand at the forefront and ensure the crowd will support itself and lead the next generation of value creation and development in our economy.

Welcome to Finance 2.0.

This is your guide.

O N E

INVESTING TODAY

———

Jack's parents lost 50% of the value in their retirement accounts in the great recession of 2008-2009. To this day, the family prepares a detailed monthly budget, accounting for the last dollar of spending while trying dollar by dollar to rebuild their lost savings. Yet the newspapers are filled with stories of Billionaire hedge fund managers who seem to make money whether the average investor wins or loses. It's hard to even know whether the smart money guys on Wall Street are actually betting against you. In fact, we learned, after the fact might I add, that many Wall Street firms were actually betting against homeowners and anticipating a crash in the real estate markets. Wall Street often seems like a casino, and a rigged casino at that. There has to be a better way to invest.

MILLENNIALS & THE STOCK MARKET

Millennials fundamentally distrust the financial markets, and I can't blame them. Whether you are 15 or 35, you have lived through at least one financial market meltdown at best and at worst three.

FINANCIAL MARKET MELTDOWNS:

1. The Great Recession of 2008
2. The Bursting of the Dot-com bubble in 2000
3. Black Monday: Stock Market Crash of 1987

We as a generation have been directly impacted by the tremendous volatility and significant downside risks of investing in our public markets. Whether directly affected or not, millennials have seen fortunes lost, pensions destroyed, and livelihoods go down the drain as a result of too much leverage being placed in the stock market. We may not have lost money ourselves, however our parents, neighbors, and relatives were all impacted, sometimes with tragic consequences.

Our generation recognizes that markets are volatile, prone to crisis, and are by no means the relatively safe haven for long term investing they were for prior generations. As such, it's become commonplace to become wary of placing a heavy emphasis on our savings in the public markets. Therefore, it is perfectly reasonable for our generation to approach investing with a skeptical lens and to look for alternatives to traditional public market investing.

Why would I put my hard earned money into something that has proven time and again to fail?

PAST PERFORMANCE ≠ THE FUTURE

"The arrogance of success is to think that what you did yesterday will be sufficient for tomorrow"

– WILLIAM POLLARD

Like it or not, experts across industry are predicting that a dollar invested in today's market is going to have to work harder than in the past to generate the same level of returns. To see anywhere near the same returns that our parents and grandparents were fortunate enough to experience, investors are going to need to become ever more savvy in navigating the public markets often seeking out alternative investing strategies. Whether we like it or not, we are entering into a period that experts predict will be marked by low growth, low yield, and higher volatility.

This new market reality is greatly different from the performance of the market for previous generations. For our parents, the answer as to how to invest for the future was simple. Even though the markets ebb and flow, no matter when you start investing in stocks, you will see your money grow over time. To date, there was little reason to question this, as even if you invested in the S&P 500 right before the 2008 crisis, your money today would still be worth more now than it was before.

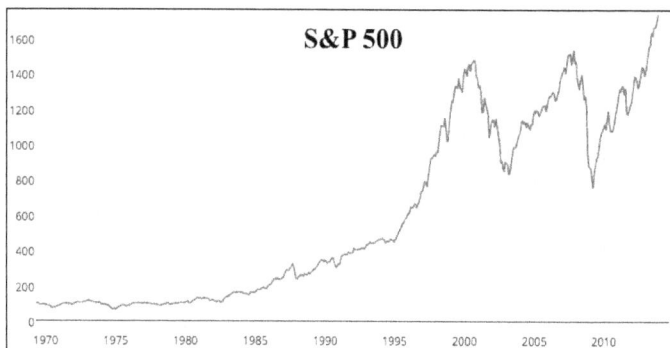

Historical S&P 500 Returns, 1950 to present

* * *

THE NEW AGE

Unfortunately, for our generation, these same historical trends that drove strong market growth for so long have started to reverse themselves. While our parents and grandparents have been able to rely upon this "Golden Principle" of investing ("Buy and Hold"), experts are predicting a far different future ahead for the public markets. While historically the market has always trended upwards, experts are now saying that we are about to head into unchartered waters.

With the market experiencing historically low yields, high volatility, and low growth prospects, many experts are saying that this trend is here to stay.

Here's what each looks like for you as an investor:

UNCHARTERED WATERS

The following charts from a recent investor presentation by noted venture capital investment firm Kleiner Perkins Caufield and Byers highlights the key headwinds limiting overall market performance.

Slower growth…

Global Real GDP Growth (%)

Generating lower yields...

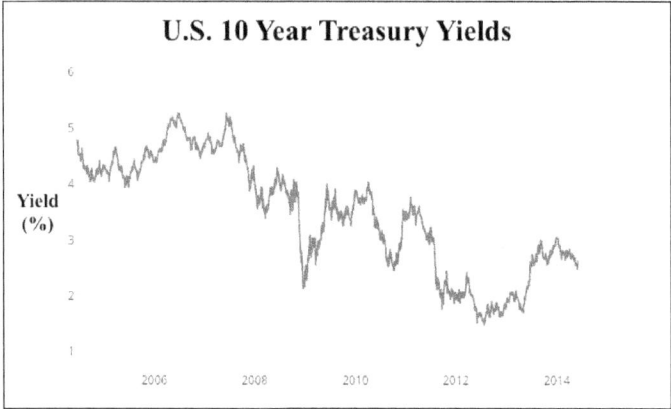

U.S. 10 Year Treasury Yields

With higher market volatility...

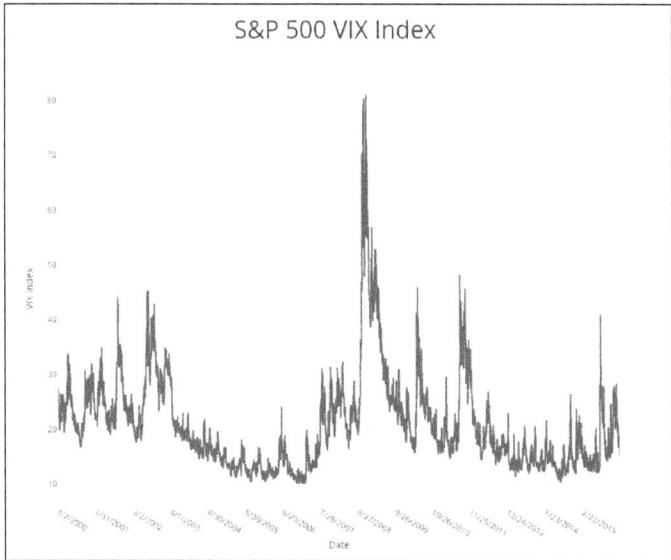

S&P 500 VIX Index

GIC, a leading global investment firm, predicts that over the next ten to twenty years we will see significantly lower returns and far more market volatility than we have ever experienced. And while our public markets may have experienced returns of 7.5% over the past thirty years, we should expect those number to drop to 4-5% moving forward. This means that market analysts and institutional investors are warier than ever before that the investment strategies they have used in the past are out of date. It is time to think differently about how to grow your money.

ALTERNATIVE INVESTMENTS: WHERE SMART MONEY GOES TO FIND RETURNS

Savvy investors have always sought out innovative opportunities to generate return on their capital: welcome to the world of alternative investments.

Alternative investments cover a broad range of investment options that typically deal with anything not falling under the typical umbrella of stocks and bonds. Alternative investments can range from hedge funds, private equity, venture capital, real estate, and real assets such as infrastructure, to more exotic tangible assets such as wine, art, timber and water.

What is most common between these investments are that they are not traded on the public markets like your typical stocks or bonds. Instead, the majority of these investments have historically been traded privately through networks of like-minded individuals.

You might ask: "aren't alternatives a rich man's game?"

In the past, these alternative investments have been closed off to the everyday investor. With access typically only granted to those who can afford it, these "country club investments " would allow the rich (net income = $1 Million+) to get richer while closing off the everyday man.

While we have seen a move towards these assets in the past, previous technology often provided a significant barrier to entry for the average investor. Fortunately, the 21st century has provided a massive shift in how the everyday investor interacts with the world around them. With technology scaling at an unprecedented rate, the barriers of the past no longer exist, allowing for tremendous opportunities today. In the end, we are seeing a seismic shift occur in how individuals invest and when all is said and done we will have a truly revolutionized investment landscape.

While many young investors today believe that one can only invest strictly in the stock market, (and while this is in fact where the majority of investment happens) there is in fact a whole world of alternative methods to invest your hard earned money.

Alternative Investments have long been a distant third cousin to traditional Stocks (Equities) and Bonds (Fixed Income) investments. Institutional Investors have long placed a small percent of their investment portfolios in these unique opportunities. This makes good sense. When you think about it, these unique types of investments often have little direct relationship with the types of return that one would see in their typical stock and bond portfolio. By spreading your money across more than just stocks and bonds and diversifying into more tangible assets such as a house or a piece of an infrastructure development, the investor is looking spread their exposure to risk.

Understanding where the risk in your investments sit is vital to making sure that you as an investor are safely growing your money. When not properly accounted for, we see fortunes lost, such as in the case of so many people who were over extended into the stock market in 2008. By having a variety of different types of investments that are not directly connected to one another, (Investment A goes up, but investment B may or may not) you are making sure you set yourself up for long term success and lower risk.

By diversifying a portfolio into alternatives, an investor is ensuring that even when their stock and bond portfolio takes a hit, they have more tangible direct investments alongside them to weaken the blow.

So what are alternative investments and why should I as a millennial care about them? Let's dive a bit deeper into the specifics of each of these alternative asset classes and touch briefly about why they pose a unique opportunity for investors.

THE BIGGEST ALTERNATIVE INVESTMENTS

Real Assets: These are "real" physical assets that have value in their actual substance and properties. Regardless of how the stock market performs there will always be tangible value in these types of investments. Whether they are real estate properties, precious metals, agriculture, machinery, oil, or infrastructure, these assets tends to be more stable than the typical financial asset.

Private Equity: These include equity investments in private companies not listed on the public stock market. Individuals can typically invest their money into private equity funds who then will go out and invest in private companies, or engage in buyouts of existing companies to create greater value.

Venture Capital: This unique type of investment allows individuals to help launch the next great companies. By investing directly into a venture capital fund, you then allow the fund to go out and invest in equity stakes (ownership) of up and coming companies, reaping the benefits of their growth.

Hedge Funds: These are unique alternative investment funds that pool investors' money and employ unique strategies to maximize your return on investment. By using derivatives, short selling, and leverage, hedge funds are often able to generate far greater returns than your typical investment vehicle.

Art, Wine, Collectible Cars and more niche alternatives: A part of the overall "real asset" investment type, these more unique investments are often done on a more individual level. As these are often harder to buy and sell, you will often see individuals invest in these unique items hoping to buy and hold on to them over a longer period of time.

* * *

Interested in investing in some of the most unique alternative investment opportunities out there?

Don't expect the process to be as easy as opening your stock brokerage account and buying a share of Apple on the stock market. These unique investment opportunities come with their own challenges to getting started investing. It is important to understand the steps it takes to get started for you as an investor to make the most out of these opportunities.

For the everyday investor, the most available opportunities are those in the niche alternatives space. Imagine that instead of investing $1,000 in stocks and bonds that you could invest in the next great piece of art or bottle of fine wine. Today for many investors that investment is a realty.

Let's take a closer look at how these investments work today:

WINE

Interested in investing in wine? Be sure to do your research before you invest in a bottle. Wine prices are often directly connected to how rare the bottle is and the quality of the wine. There are a variety of online platforms that will show you the top "investment grade" wines to add to your collection. Before you invest you should also be sure to look into the wine stock market: The Liv-Ex or London International Vintners Exchange, a global trading platform for fine wine merchants. Savvy investors can sort through and find their next great bottle of wine or use their platform's Fine Wine 100 Index to see how the top investment grade wine prices have shifted over time.

ART

Art as an investment has exploded in recent years with investors hoping to find and add the next great up and coming artist to their collection. As demand has skyrocketed, so too have we seen the prices of some of the most popular categories of art.

Investors hoping to add art to their investment portfolio should be keen on looking out for local auctions and art fairs, as they are often the place to find the most unique offering for the best value. The digitally enabled investor can turn to online auction houses and art fairs such as SaatchiArt.com or AffordableArtFair. com. Investors can then sift through and find works of art to add to their collection with listed pieces starting as low as $100.

COLLECTIBLE CARS

One of the most common luxury investments that we see the everyday man enter into is the purchase of a great classic car. What better way to benefit from putting your hard earned money to work then being able to enjoy a collectible car that may also accrue in value over time. However, for the savviest car collectors finding the perfect investment is far more than a minor hobby. As the most in demand and out of stock cars can skyrocket in value, finding the perfect "diamond in the rough" is the goal of most investors. Finding a great value in a collectible car can be tough, but investors are often keen to keep tabs on the most popular makes, models, and vintages of cars over the years. Your best bet to finding a great car to invest in is typically a car auction or online marketplace. Some investors are even looking to the future and already investing in cars like such as the DeLorean DMC 12 made famous in "Back to The Future" in hopes of having it someday be worth far more than the $30,000 they cost today.

ALTERNATIVES

Two of the more unique "tangible" investment opportunities that we are seeing investors enter into are timber and water. While not as flashy as being able to show off your new 1955 Ford Thunderbird or the work of the next Warhol, these investments prove a value of their own, allowing the investor a benefit that often spans far greater than merely financially over time.

TIMBER

Investing in timber (or wood), gives investors the ability to diversify their investments into a unique and far more tangible asset then merely a stock certificate. For timber investors, their investment is in physical pieces of land that have growing trees (timber) on them. The goal of these investors is to allow for their assets (the trees) to grow over time, hopefully having the value of timber grow alongside it. For these investors, their return is often a collection of 1) the value of timber increasing, 2) the amount of timber (biological growth), and 3) land appreciation. As timber requires physical land to grow, timber investors are able to experience the unique benefit of owning a potentially large plot of forest land (try being able to hunt or fish with your stock market investments).

Those interested in entering into timber investments can either easily invest in public timber REITs (Real Estate Investment

Trusts) or go out and purchase timber land themselves. The REIT option allows for the investor to more easily invest in the timber, but hold less upside then owning the land yourself. The second option of owning your own land, while more tedious, can prove far more fruitful if done correctly. Those interested in pursuing their own properties of timber can even hire Timber Investment Management Organizations (TIMOs) to purchase and manage their timber for them.

WATER

Similar to investing in timber, many investors today are looking to invest directly in and around water as an asset. Whether it is investing in what are called "water rights" (the ability to use fresh water), investing in water-rich farmland, or in water infrastructure, many investors are looking to win big on the asset we all often take for granted.

Take Dr. Michael Burry, the investor made famous for his successful prediction of the 2008 housing and credit collapse through the movie The Big Short. In the late 2000s Michael Burry won big on investing against Wall Street, today he has his sights set on a different target: water.

"Michael Burry is focusing all of his trading on one commodity: Water"

– THE BIG SHORT

All in all, while these various "real" investments can provide a unique benefit to investors over time, they too hold their own unique risks. Without a fluid market like the public stock market in place for these various investments, it is often difficult for investors to a) find well priced investments to make and b) a fair buyer to take the goods off their hands when they are ready to sell their investment. As such, investors in these more unique alternative investments often need to understand that their money will be locked up in the investment for five to seven years before they will be able to see a return.

TWO

A FINTECH REVOLUTION

———

"Silicon Valley is coming. There are hundreds of start-ups with a lot of brains and money working on various alternatives to traditional banking."

– JAMIE DIMON, CEO – JP MORGAN CHASE

When Vladimir Tevev and Baiju Bhatt first met at Stanford in 2004, they could little predict the impact they were about to have on reshaping the future of financial services. At the time, the two were undergrads at Stanford studying math. And while the two would not follow in the footsteps of the many Stanford undergrads before them that would start a business while in school, they would later carry on the same innovative spirit that echoes from the Santa Clara campus.

The movement that they were about to launch would far surpass anything that they could have dreamt of during their undergraduate days.

While Vladimir would go on to continue studying math at U.C.L.A., Baiju decided to explore the illustrious world of Wall Street finance. Designing technology platforms for some of the most successful hedge funds of the time, he learned the ins and outs of the emerging world of high frequency trading. Specifically, he began learning how these large global financial institutions were leveraging complex algorithmic trading to generate unprecedented profits.

When the 2008 crisis hit, few truly understood exactly what had happened. Everyone was left scrambling to understand how the most economically prosperous times for Wall Street had crashed so quickly. Having lived directly in this world for the last four years, Baiju saw first hand how the institutions were able to crumble so quickly. Leveraging his entrepreneurial ingenuity, he saw an opportunity to reshape this heavily outdated world of financial services.

Reconnecting with his former Stanford peer Vladimir, the two set out to build a solution that they thought could truly shake up the outdated world of finance.

Enter Robinhood.

What Baiju saw firsthand in building high frequency trading platforms for hedge funds was that the cost of transacting a single trade was so minimal that it would barely leave a mark on these institutions. Instead, these financial behemoths were able to execute thousands of trades in a given second to profit off of any minor inefficiencies they saw in the markets.

While he saw no cost to the large firms he was working with, he saw the E-Trade's and Charles Schwab's of the world charging every day investors upwards of $7.99 just to buy a single stock.

"Could we do something better than this?"

– BAIJU BHATT, CO-FOUNDER, ROBINHOOD

The two believed that they could create a more efficient service for enabling the average retail investor to shape a better picture for how the future of America and the world was able to trade and invest in the stock market. What they built was an innovative platform that reduced the fees of trading a stock to zero for the individual.

"Robinhood doesn't charge anything per trade. It's a free stock brokerage"

– BAIJU BHATT

By opening up the public markets to the average investor they hoped to even the playing field for the everyday man.

In an industry known for cutting out the lowest man on the totem pole Robinhood "wanted to build a platform that stood for the everyday consumer." – Vladamir Tenev, Co-Founder & CEO, Robinhood

Today their platform, justly named Robinhood, has over 1 million users, $12 Billion in trades transacted, and has saved consumers over $200 million in fees, serving as a just reminder to the value that our innovators have in reshaping our day-to-day lives.

But Vladimir and Baiju are just the tip of the massive wave of people looking to shakeup the world of finance. By taking the same approach that transformative innovators have had across so many other sectors, they are retooling how our society manages money and transacts in the markets at the most fundamental level.

"In ten years, people might think it's crazy we used to pay to trade stocks when all it takes is a few taps."

– JOSH CONSTINE, TECHCRUNCH

* * *

Welcome to the FinTech Revolution.

What is FinTech?

FinTech, or Financial Technology, involves the variety of companies looking to shake up financial services by leveraging technology to create new markets, connect individuals with investment opportunities, and educate and empower retail investors to take charge of their financial resources. These entrepreneurs are utilizing innovative technology to design and deliver the next generation of financial solutions. Today they are transforming the banking sector and forever reshaping how the everyday individual looks at and interacts with their financial world.

In just the 3rd quarter of 2016 in North America alone, over $2.4 Billion was invested in some 178 individual companies in the FinTech space. According to KPMG and H2 Ventures, the scope of global FinTech financing has risen over seven times over the past three years, to reach an estimated $20 billion in 2015. To put this into perspective, that's a 66 percent increase in the level of FinTech investment between 2014 and last year. FinTech is one of the hottest sectors for both start-ups and venture investors. Capital is flowing into innovative companies that are seeking to disrupt the global financial services industry. The gold rush is on!

THE NEXT WAVE

We are living in one of the greatest entrepreneurial revolutions in all of human history. When two individuals can sit down in a garage and flush out the next billion-dollar business idea, you know our competitive environment has greatly changed. As we have seen time and time again, technology is reshaping how our world and economy operates. When Uber can take over the entire taxi industry without owning a single car and AirBnb can reshape how hospitality is done without owning a single property, we have learned to understand that there is tremendous value in technological disruption.

The same is holding true for the financial services industry. Where historically we look at only the biggest banks as holding the ability to leverage the wealth of so many, today we are seeing technology open up some of the most innovative financial tools to investors at lower costs and lower amounts.

Across the board, we are seeing a FinTech revolution begin to surge over our entire global ecosystem.

From artificial intelligence to Blockchain to robo-advisors, peer-to-peer lending, crowdfunding, and big data, the emergence of so many unique outlets mean that the possibilities are endless for how the innovators of tomorrow can reshape how individuals interact with their finances.

The outbreak of FinTech means that finance as we know it is changing at a fundamental level. While in the past we may have seen the big banks hold the keys to generating innovative solutions for the everyday consumer, today we are seeing these behemoths of power become ever more fragmented.

When the founder of Twitter, Jack Dorsey, launched Square in 2007, he had little idea how much of an impact it was going to make in the overall world of credit card transactions. Nevertheless, today, Square finds itself transacting over $10 billion in Q1 2016 alone among stores across the world and has grown to a valuation of over $5 billion.

"FinTech companies are undoubtedly having a movement, [they] are everywhere."

– MCKINSEY & COMPANY ON FINANCIAL TECHNOLOGY

AN OLD MONEY SHAKEUP: WEALTH MANAGEMENT 2.0

As long as these banks have been in business, high net worth individuals, those with over $1 million plus of assets, have looked to financial advisors to manage their wealth. This industry, known as wealth management, has long been a key building block of how these banks generate revenue. However, we are similarly seeing a fundamental shift in how the everyday investor interacts with their wealth manager and their financial advisors.

Already major platforms such as WealthFront and Betterment are taking over the business of many outdated advisors. By looking to take a more passive approach to investing, these digital advisors see a tremendous value in finding automated solutions, requiring less manpower, to generate investment portfolios for their clients.

"Today, banks are in a fight for the customer, not only with other banks but also non-banks."

– MCKINSEY & COMPANY

By auto-managing portfolios based on investors' risk tolerance and return objectives, these companies are able to streamline their processes and reduce the massive overhead costs these banks have had to deal with. Without the need for thousands of physical financial advisors managing one-on-one client relationships, these financial innovators are able to streamline costs for the end user, the investor.

THE MILLENNIAL TAKE

As millennials, we care far more about earning an efficient return our money than having to spend money on countless fees and dealing with the countless headaches of the typical bank. At the most basic level, we as a generation are constantly looking to find an easier way to deal with our finances.

When I understand that I can put the $1,000 I earned in my job into a WealthFront or Betterment account, knowing full well that it is being managed by some of the brightest minds in finance, I am far more confident in the safety of those investments, than were I merely to turn to the local Charles Schwab advisor's generic investment advice.

We are seeing this same kind of seismic shift occur in the most fundamental forms of investment types for individuals as well. As the FinTech revolution has pushed into consumer lending, we have seen massive entities such as Lending Club and Prosper thrive in reshaping how individuals lend to one another.

So much so that Lending Club has recently gone public and currently has a valuation of over $2 billion. Their platform is reshaping how individuals reach out to their peers and opening up an entire new world of investment opportunities to the everyday investor.

We have already seen the impact that technology can have across a variety of different industries. Whether it is transportation, hospitality, or investing, when the innovators of today are given an opportunity to address the problems of tomorrow, there is the opportunity for tremendous value creation.

"We're witnessing the creative destruction of financial services, rearranging itself around the consumer. Who does this in the most relevant, exciting way using data and digital, wins!"

- ARVIND SANKARAN, SENIOR ADVISOR
— MCKINSEY & COMPANY

* * *

The floodgates have opened for finance to be reshaped. For too long the powers at be have held the financial services sector in far too few entities. As we have seen through the Occupy Wall Street movement and countless others, there is a fundamental desire to democratize the financial services world.

The FinTech revolution is one that will fundamentally reshape the everyday lives of individuals. The entrepreneurs of today are ensuring that the most innovative solutions are being addressed in terms of how the everyday investor deals with their finances. Each and every day they are finding new and innovative ways to create value for the everyday individual. They are reshaping everything about how businesses and individuals seek loans and raise money from how individuals seek loans to raise how businesses raise money with the future possibilities being virtually endless. What we can be sure of is that these solutions will redesign our world.

THREE

THE NEW SHARING ECONOMY

——

"LAST night 40,000 people rented accommodation from a service that offers 250,000 rooms in 30,000 cities in 192 countries. They chose their rooms and paid for everything online. But their beds were provided by private individuals, rather than a hotel chain. Hosts and guests were matched up by Airbnb, a firm based in San Francisco. Since its launch in 2008 more than 4m people have used it—2.5m of them in 2012 alone. It is the most prominent example of a huge new "sharing economy", in which people rent beds, cars, boats and other assets directly from each other, co-ordinated via the internet."

– THE ECONOMIST "THE RISE OF THE SHARING ECONOMY"

* * *

Our generation is writing a new set of rules for the economy. Why own something when you can share? Market analysts call it the Sharing Economy and it is impacting all major segments of the economy.

Why buy a car when you can *Uber*?

Want to share your car with your neighbor? Try Google backed *RelayRides*!

Going out of town? Forget the hotel and go with *Airbnb*!

Don't own a bike but want to go for a ride? Try the bike sharing service called *LiquidNeed*!

Need to borrow some money? Simply have a friend *Venmo* you a few dollars!

At every turn we are seeing smart companies innovate using technology to increase efficiencies and let individuals transact directly with one another, all the while creating jobs and disrupting sector after sector of the traditional economy.

"As people's access to the internet grows we're seeing the sharing economy boom – I think our obsession with ownership is at the

tipping point and the sharing economy is part of the antidote for that."

– RICHARD BRANSON, FOUNDER OF THE VIRGIN GROUP

While in the past, consumers purchased goods for their own individual use, we are at the forefront of a massive shift in how individuals seek to not capture as many resources for themselves, but instead begin to share resources with one another.

This collective "sharing economy" is taking off far quicker and far larger than anyone could have possibly imagined. First and foremost, we can see the success of AirBnb and Uber in showing just how valuable and impactful this new consumer mindset can be; that it is more helpful and valuable to share with peers than to hold it wholly for one's own use.

Instead of the average consumer buying a vacation home in Florida or owning a car in a city, they are now able to share the cost with their peers and only pay for what they need. They can use someone else's home or car, in the case of AirBnb or Uber. Many of today's consumers believe that this approach makes the most effective use of their money and the most efficient use of their time.

The Sharing Economy is beginning to change the face of investing. The impact of the sharing economy is far and wide as we see a fundamental shift in consumers being far more open to investing alongside their peers than directly against them.

Millennial's see tremendous value in pulling resources together especially when it can be around a common vision.

It is truly remarkable when you are able to rally your friends around a common idea and push forward tremendous value creation.

* * *

We are similarly seeing this sharing economic mindset spreading into the world of investing.

Welcome to the world of Alternative Finance.

Alternative finance encompasses the emerging world of investing in next generation of assets. In the past these alternative investments were closed off to the average investor, never able to reap the benefits that their wealthier counterparts could experience. This new world of alternative finance however is opening up this tremendous wealth of opportunity in chunks as small as $100 to the everyday investor.

Whether you want to invest in the next big real estate project, pools of prime credit (previously exclusive to the major banks), or equity in the next great early stage company, alternative finance is allowing the next generation of investors to invest alongside their peers in order to make a lasting change in our communities.

Enter Crowdfunding.

As individuals see far more value in the ability to invest alongside their peers or with the "crowd" there has been a tremendous opportunity created in the process.

What is Crowdfunding?

Crowdfunding takes the idea of a sharing economy and opens it up to the masses. Specifically, it opens it up to individuals who are looking to invest behind an idea. What it does is takes and pools the money of countless individuals, upwards of thousands at a time, and pools it around a common goal. Each member investing in the idea puts a small amount of money behind it in order to collectively create a far larger ripple effect. In the end, by each member adding a small piece to the overall puzzle, the company or vision behind the idea is able to experience a far greater impact.

CROWDFUNDING LADY LIBERTY

Let's take a look back and one of the earliest accounts of crowdfunding in American history. While it should hold close to most American's hearts, it is also one of the most easily forgotten.

In the summer of 1885, the pieces of the The Statue of Liberty had arrived in New York City waiting to be assembled. While the statue itself was a gift from the French, the people of New York needed to build a proper pedestal to display their newly received gift. The problem for New Yorkers was that then New York Governor Grover Cleveland rejected the use of city funds to build a base for the statue. With the production of the Statue of Liberty halted and many New Yorkers fearing that another city would step up to claim the statue, the city needed a way to find the funds fast.

A man by the name of Joseph Pulitzer decided to take initiative and lead the charge on bringing the funds needed to complete production together. Leveraging the technology of the time, he decided to use his newspaper, The New York World, to launch a national fundraising campaign. With the hope of reaching Americans across the country, Pulitzer hoped to unite Americans far and wide and push the development over the finish line. Whether they could donate one penny or one hundred dollars Pulitzer pleaded with American's to donate as much as they could for the cause.

Eventually raising money from more than 160,000 donors ranging from businessmen, to young children and street workers, the campaign was able to raise $101,091 to cover the $100,000 needed to complete the pedestal. All the more amazing, more than three-quarters of the donations towards the cause were less than one dollar, a true testament to the value of the crowd.

Today the Statue of Liberty stands as an icon of American freedom and prosperity. Little did we know that it too had some of the deepest roots to the crowdfunding movement that we are seeing take off today.

"Every American should feel proud to donate to The Pedestal Fund and own a Model in token of their subscription and proof of title to ownership in this great work."

- THE NEW YORK WORLD, "LIBERTY ENLIGHTENING THE WORLD" - ISSUED BY THE AMERICAN COMMITTEE IN AID OF THE PEDESTAL FUND

* * *

Just as there are various types of ways of raising money for businesses of all stages, there are a variety of different methods of crowdfunding. In order to best understand the intricate world of crowdfunding, let's look at a breakdown of the key types:

Donation-Based Crowdfunding: Allows individuals to donate along with their peers towards a given cause. Typically, these sorts of crowdfunding campaigns will be used to benefit a charity or non-profit as the money you put towards the project is not rewarded in any way and as such is seen as a "donation".

Rewards-Based Crowdfunding: Allows individuals to donate to unique up and coming projects in exchange for non-monetary "rewards". Often the types of people and businesses that look to launch a rewards-based crowdfunding campaign are at the early stages of their idea and need money to get started with. Instead of any financial return, the "supporters" of these projects often receive a tweet, t-shirt, or early adoption of the product.

Equity-Based Crowdfunding: Allows people to invest in businesses that are looking to raise money in exchange for an ownership stake of their company. Unlike rewards-based crowdfunding, equity crowdfunding allows investors to buy into a piece of a company and see long term benefits as that company grows.

Debt-Based Crowdfunding: Allows investors to loan out money along with their peers to individuals and businesses who are looking for funding. Whether it is to refinance student loans, a new mortgage, or a small business loan to expand operations, debt-based crowdfunding allows for investors to earn a more fixed and steady return on their investment into individual people and businesses.

* * *

As we see above, this model of pooling money from the crowd has been tremendously successful for both the nonprofit as well as the consumer side. When charities are able to pool together their supporters in small chunks of change they are able to push forward a greater larger than any one individual could possibly have imagined.

Similarly, we see another great example of the power of crowdfunding through Kickstarter's explosive success.

Kickstarter started several years ago with the idea that entrepreneurs could launch an idea and gain the support of their peers by raising money from their colleagues.

How does Kickstarter work?

An entrepreneur starts by putting up a page for his or her project. From there, it is up to them to pitch their idea to the masses and reward those who donate to their campaign. With prizes ranging from social media recognition to a T-shirt or early product prototype, the entrepreneur is able to create a movement behind their product and rally a network of supporters.

"Kickstarter isn't a profit center, it's an organizer and an instigator"

– SETH GODIN, BEST SELLING AUTHOR WHO SUCCESSFULLY LAUNCHED FOUR BOOKS ON KICKSTARTER

This collection of consumer's insights around a vision allows people to vote for the next great idea with their wallet, helping launch them off the ground. Ideas that may have not been able to get off the ground for lack of funding or lack of other resources are able to be propelled forward with the help of these real world backers.

"The combination of having a great video, a lot more access to people through Twitter, and having Kickstarter be this new thing in. We tapped into it, at its inception, and got people interested in it just based on the concept of what Kickstarter was. The timing was right."

– SIMON HELBERG, STAR OF THE BIG BANG THEORY, SUCCESSFULLY RAISED OVER $110,000 ON KICKSTARTER TO FINANCE THE FILM "I AM I".

AN EARLY KICKSTARTER SUCCESS

Meet twenty-year-old entrepreneur Palmer Luckey.

"I'm a self-taught engineer, a hacker, an electronic enthusiast. I'm from Long Beach, California. My dad was a car salesman. My mom was a stay-at-home mom. I like making things"

"I'm a pretty regular Joe"

From an early age, Palmer Luckey had been interested in video games. He specifically was fascinated in the unique ways that he could interact with the games he grew up playing. Discovering the world of virtual reality (VR), Palmer began building and modifying his own head-mounted displays to use for his video games. By sourcing the parts himself and building out his displays from his garage, he began to hone his craft and expertise. He even began to develop a reputation amongst the niche VR community online, going so far as to connect with and send one of his early units to legendary id Software programmer John Carmack.

However, when Palmer wanted to scale his idea, he soon realized that he would need to source far more parts than he had hoped for in order to cut down his cost of producing a larger quantity.

"My plan was to do a Kickstarter for about 100 of these things

- basically, to get money to buy all of the components required on a slightly larger scale and then send these out to people as kits so they could assemble them themselves using my instructions so they could have the same thing as I had."

Originally thinking that he would only get a couple "VR nerds" on board Palmer launched his Kickstarter with a goal of $250,000. He would soon realize that he would be in for far more than he bargained for. The original goal of only building 100 units would soon be in the rear-view mirror as his Kickstarter exploded raising over $670,000 from 2,750 people in just 24 hours. In just 30 short days Palmer Luckey's Kickstarter campaign, Oculus Rift, raised almost $2,500,000 from over 9,500 individuals.

"I started to realize that it wasn't just going to be a successful Kickstarter - it was going to be one of the more successful Kickstarters out there."

Oculus would later go to raise an additional $2.55 million dollars in seed funding the next month, starting a snowball effect that allowed the business to grow at an unprecedented rate. Over the next two years Oculus went on to raise an additional $81 million collectively in a series A and B funding round. It eventually went on to sell for $2 billion in March of 2014 to Facebook, making a statement to the world that the virtual reality age was upon us.

What may have originally been a hobby for Palmer Luckey hoping to find 40-50 other virtual reality enthusiasts was quickly a distant memory as his company began to take over the emerging world of virtual reality.

Kickstarter was the spark plug that Luckey needed to ignite a transformation in not only his life, but the entire industry of virtual reality. Helping lead the charge with Oculus, the company is now at the forefront of all things virtual reality, leading innovation in one of the fastest growing tech industries today.

* * *

WHEN REWARDS ARE NOT ENOUGH

In the past, the downside to Kickstarter has been that the only reward the investor could reap would be early adoption of a product, a T-shirt, or a tweet from their founders. While fantastic for the early adopter who wants the product, it limits this individual's ability to really invest behind the idea with a true monetary bonus if they in fact see it as being the next great idea.

Where venture capitalists could buy into an idea early on putting a small chunk of money behind one that they believe in, these investors are closed off and cannot benefit in the same way.

However, what we have been able to see is that the FinTech movement that has transformed how individuals pay and operate their mobile banking is similarly impacting the massive world of alternative investments.

Where in the past these private investments in early stage companies would have been limited to the venture capital firms the world. What we are seeing is the ability to take the multi-million dollar check that a venture capitalist would write to a company and divvy it up into smaller and smaller chunks, opening up those shares up to the masses in increments as low as $100.

What that means is that equivalents to Kickstarter are opening up where instead of receiving a t-shirt for your monetary backing, you receive a portion of equity in the company.

The two biggest components of this emerging alternative finance space are peer-to-peer lending and equity crowdfunding. While each encompassing the crowdinvesting vision, they too push forward their own unique approach to how the crowd can reshape the investing world.

Peer-to-Peer Lending: Allows you, as investors, to pool your money together and help fund the loans of individuals and businesses who are looking for money. By opening up these loans to the crowd, we, as investors, are able to buy bits and pieces of a variety of different types of loans and earn a good return, all while helping out those who may need the money most.

Equity Crowdfunding: Allows you as an investor to invest in chunks as small as $100 into private companies that are looking for money to grow. By investing your money in exchange for a real piece of the company (equity) you buy yourself a seat on the future success of the company, opening yourself to far greater return than the typical stock.

This idea of "crowd-investing" is reshaping how individuals and businesses look at their everyday finances. Now instead of needing to go to a big bank to raise money you are able to turn to your peers in the "crowd" for help.

While for so long we have seen the world of alternative investments closed off to the everyday investor, today's entrepreneurial revolution is allowing the innovators tomorrow to open up our world in new and ever-changing ways. We are seeing a seismic shift in how the everyday investor can interact with the global economy.

Just as the sharing economy has transformed traditional markets with the Airbnb's and Uber's of the world, there is about to be a massive shift in how the everyday investor interacts and it invests in the world around them. We are just at the beginning to this movement. It's certainly time to take note. Because the world of investments as we know it is about to change for the better. Alternative finance is not about to come and go, instead this alternative form of investment may be the new mainstream.

FOUR

A PEER TO PEER REVOLUTION

———

Did you take out any loans to pay for your education? Join the club. Americans owe nearly $1.3 trillion in student loan debt.

Have you ever used a credit card to purchase something you could not immediately buy from your savings? You are not alone. Outstanding U.S. Consumer Debt: totals some $3.4 trillion. Thinking about borrowing money to start a business? The Small Business Administration reports there are nearly $600 billion in small business loans outstanding. And let's not forget the granddaddy of them all, real estate. Thinking of borrowing to buy a home? The New York Fed reports that as of Q1 consumers owed some $8.37 trillion in real estate loans.

Whether you need a mortgage to buy your first home, a loan to pay off your credit card bills, or a student loan to be able to college, few people today are able to do so with the savings they have in their bank. Instead, what many need to do is go to their local banks and get a loan that they are able to pay off over time to support their lifestyle. Realizing the American Dream has long been powered by ready access to loans to fund a range of purchases. Some might say that the American Dream is built on some form of borrowing.

We all can relate to the need to have access to loans. I am sure the reality is no different for you, the reader of this book.

Recent changes on banking regulations have made it far more difficult for the average consumer to secure the same loans he could once afford. As the regulatory requirements placed on lenders increases, it has become harder and harder for the average American to access credit.

Limits on access to credit has impacted growth in the economy as well as the day to day living of many consumers. Lately it's gotten harder and harder for those same Americans to afford the quality of life that they had the past. It is getting harder to secure the loan for a new car, to buy a larger television, or even take that vacation to Disney. With the stock markets experiencing more volatility than ever before and the interest rates on savings accounts being at all-time lows, the ability for consumers to access affordable loans is getting more important.

Fortunately, creative visionaries are leveraging technology to improve the efficiency, expand the reach for potential lenders, and enable consumers to access the additional credit they need. In doing so, marketplaces are evolving that directly connect individuals creating an environment where at any given time one can be either a borrower or a lender. Direct peer-to-peer lending is now a growing element in the Sharing Economy, creating yet another example of technology disrupting an existing set of established intermediaries.

You experienced this type of disruptive disintermediation first-hand in how you received this book. As we all know, Amazon has opened the floodgates for small publishers and changed the way that consumers interact with their digital and print media. No longer does an individual need to march down to their local Barnes and Noble or Borders to pick up the next bestseller. Instead, they can turn on the computer flip through Amazon's website and browse far more books than any one bookstore could possibly hold.

The ease of the access to content suddenly means that instead of aspiring authors needing to push through the bureaucracy of getting an editor and a publisher to agree to support and promote their work, they instead can publish their thoughts directly to a reader on a Kindle.

In this digital age it is not the distributor who drives the content that is shared with the consumer, but instead the reins lie with the consumers themselves. Whether you sell ten copies or ten thousand copies, the authors themselves are able to get in front of their audience and share their thoughts of the world.

Just as we have seen the tremendous changes that have accompanied Internet in the publishing industry, we are seeing the same happen to one of the largest sectors of the global economy, credit.

By side-stepping the intermediates (the banks) this next wave of lending will facilitate a more intimate relationship between the individual and the borrower. No longer does the family of five looking for a loan have to go to the big bank to do so. Instead, they can look to innovative credit marketplaces such as Lending Club or Prosper in order to raise the funds.

Through a collective pooling of individuals who believe in their story and believe in their ability to pay back the loan, both the borrower and lenders can benefit.

This new ecosystem means that a lender in Chicago can contribute to a loan to help raise money for a small business in Jacksonville with knowledge and understanding that they'll be returning their money with more than a good enough return.

This is a fundamental shift in the mindset of the consumer interacting with investing.

Where in the past we see individuals place their money in the stock market or elsewhere with little direct involvement, today there can be more of a direct connection between the investor and the investment.

The next generation of investors can now lend directly into someone's story and buy into the vision for their future growth and prospects. This enables a healthier kind of economy where we can co-exist and co-invest in one another throughout the belief that helping with your local economy will do more to spur growth.

In the face of our great recession where we saw so much financial scandal, this new model presents a breath of fresh air for investors. We can not only see a strong return on our investment but also recognize that a significant social impact is being made. In doing so, we better understand the need to invest directly back into our economy.

This peer-to-peer revolution has experienced tremendous growth in recent years. With a variety of major platforms out there leading the charge we are seeing a new wave of demand for this unique investment opportunity.

Today we are seeing individuals with the proper credit receiving rates that they otherwise might not have been able to secure from a traditional bank.

* * *

AN OVERVIEW

Peer to peer lending is unique in that there is a certain social aspect to participating. It is one of the few places where you as an investor can turn and put your money to work directly back into the community around you, all while still earning a great return.

It is this unique social benefit that not only helps you but helps the community at large that truly separates it from nearly any other form of investment. While at times the concept of peer to peer lending can get complex, let's take a quick bird's eye view of how the entire process works:

BORROWERS:

From the start, a borrower will go to one of the platforms such as, Prosper, Lending Club, or Funding Circle looking for a loan. In order to be eligible to receive a loan, the potential borrower will need to share some of their background information with the platform. Information such as the borrower's social security number and employment status will allow the site to perform the necessary due diligence to vet the applicant. Next if their loan gets approved for the platform (typically only 10% of those who apply do), their loan request is then is placed on the platform for a period of two weeks to seek funding. During these two weeks any potential investor can browse through the available loans on the platform and choose which one's that would like to invest behind. If the borrower's loan reaches the amount requested within those two weeks, their loan is moved on to final approval by the platform itself. The borrower then proceeds to repay their loan over time (plus interest) in the form of monthly payments. This continues on until the borrower has fully paid off the balance of the loan received through the platform. Part of the payment includes a fee for the platform, which is effectively paid by the borrower.

INVESTORS:

From the lenders side the process is fairly simple. You first need to submit an application and become approved as a lender (this must be done for each platform you intend to use). After becoming an approved lender all you need to do is go on to the platforms and connect your bank account to transfer funds into your lending account to be able to manage from there. You are then freely able to go through the loans currently listed on the platform and pick and choose which ones you'd like to invest your money behind. For each of the thousands of loans on a given platform you are able to dig deeper into the specific financial background of the person seeking the loan, giving you as the investor a greater peace of mind as to where your money is going.

"How can you tell which loans are the best?"

- SIMON CUNNINGHAM, LENDINGMEMO

As Simon Cunningham puts it, you can not possibly be sure that a loan will be repaid due to the fact that there is another real person on the other side of the platform. You as an investor will never be able to fully account for the situations they may face over time. Repayment risk is always something a lender must consider when deciding to make a loan. The nature of these peer-to-peer platforms, however, is that these loans are essentially backed by the platforms that host them. As such, these loans have already been prescreened to a certain extent and ensured of a certain quality of risk before they are open to you, the public investor. As a result, you can take some comfort in that you're not blindly dealing with the riskiest loans of which may not have the slightest chance of getting paid back without properly getting compensated for your risk. But let's be clear, direct lending maintains risk.

To assist in your search for loans that meet your requirements, many platforms have developed a process to help you separate out the loans that meet your investment criteria from those that do not. This custom search function allows you as an investor to divvy up to the loans through a process called filtering. These filters allow you to sort through a variety of different factors relating to the potential borrower. While at first this process may seem tedious and complex, over time you as an investor will be able to quickly hone your filtering skills. As your expertise grows you will be able to more successfully determine the exact qualifications you'd like to find in loans and find the specific loans that you as an investor want put your money back.

It takes time to develop the best practices of sorting through and finding the best loans in which to invest. As your cash slowly trickles in on a month-to-month basis, being able to reinvest your earnings into other loans allows you to ensure that you are maximizing your overall returns.

All in all, it is fairly straightforward to begin investing in the world of peer-to-peer loans. By building a basic lending account and investing your money in the simplest types of loans, you can see returns upwards of 5%. As you get more advanced in your ability to filter loans and know what to look for in the best loans many people have experienced returns reaching 8-9%.

In the end, getting more specialized with finding the right loans will take some time. It is important to begin with the basics and do not dive in too quickly as it will be important to develop your expertise over time. What follows will be a basic guideline of some of the strategies that many investors in the peer to peer space used to find the best loans and as well as advice on learning the ins and outs of this exciting investment opportunity.

* * *

THE INVESTMENT PROCESS

Peer to peer lending platforms make it easy for the user to go from no loans to investing in multiple loans in a quick period of time. By following the next four steps, we can guide you through the process of going from creating a new account to investing across a variety of peer to peer notes.

While the process that follows is by no means an exact science, it should give you, as an investor, a good set of guidelines for how to get started in the peer-to-peer investing world.

1) UNDERSTAND THE HEALTH OF YOUR ACCOUNT

After logging in to your account on whatever site you choose (Lending Club, Prosper, and Funding Circle being the top few) you will want to go to your main account dashboard (this will be where you access the vital information about your account). This page will show many of the key facts of your account and your historical performance. Over time you are going to learn to have this page be a key part of your routine in investing in peer to peer loan as it shows that the main attributes of your progress over time and can track your investment results.

From here you will want to examine your account and see how you stand. Below are a few of the key performing indicators that will show your progress.

Return on Investment (ROI): This will show you how your account has performed to date. It is a key measurement of the success of your peer to peer investments and will be an easy gauge to see how your money is growing over time.

Available Cash: Your available cash to invest will show you the money that is connected to your account and freely able to be used to invest. This amount will increase over time as loans are repaid. It is important to make sure this number stays as low as possible to ensure that you are earning the best possible return on your money. As peer to peer platforms to date will not let you generate interest off of the money that is sitting in your account, this money is in theory losing value as you let it sit passive in your account.

Total Account Value: This is the total value of your account. It included the amount of money that you have loaned out (funds locked up in loans) + the available cash you have to reinvest. This number is important to understand as you better gauge the amount of your overall savings that you are looking to invest in peer-to-peer loans.

Overall these three give you a good indicator of the health of your account and how your track record has been overall. As you begin to progress with your peer to peer investments you'll hopefully see your return on investment grow over time as you receive successful payments on your notes. Similarly, it is crucial to look at your available cash on hand as the platform. Since these platforms do not allow you to receive interest on this money, by not reinvesting these funds you are losing out on potential returns.

Once you have a good sense for the health of your account you are next going to want to understand how much money you have to invest and then go out and look for available loans.

2) BROWSE AND FILTER AVAILABLE LOANS

In looking for available loans you will be exposed to thousands of potential loans at a given platform. Early on this process can seen to be a daunting challenge as you don't know what to look for in each loan and the risk that each poses for your money. But fortunately, as we mentioned before, these platforms have developed over time to allow you to pick and choose criteria otherwise known as filters to find the loans that most fit your investment needs.

When you start browsing through thousands of options you are going to want to start filtering out these notes. After you become experienced with a given platform you are able to save these filters and save search results to speed the process up getting back to exactly the type of loans that you've invested in previously. Each peer to peer investor has a unique take on the type of loans and the type of risk that they want to be exposed to. Later on in this chapter we will dive deep into some basic filters that people have used and why they use them as well as help you start to build your own expertise in terms of finding filters and building out filters that you want to start sifting through these loans.

3) EXAMINE AND INVEST IN NOTES

After isolating the specific notes that you want to target through filtering, you are going to want to start closer examining the loans that are listed under the search. As there will still be a large number of loans here it is time to make sure that they all add up to your criteria. At times you may find that the criteria you had in place, whether it's the amount of work experience or credit score, does not line perfectly in place when you inspect a given loan. Therefore, it is important to look at the details of the loans that come up to ensure that in fact all of the base criteria for your filters that have been thought out and narrowed out.

From there it's important to look at some of the other information about the specific loan and make sure that you can believe that you can buy into the story behind the borrower. While filtering out with a base criterion gives you a good sense of the loans you want to invest in, ultimately you have a limited amount of money to invest so you as an investor want to make sure you are picking the loans you see as strongest for potential returns.

Once you found those loans you want to invest in it is time to put your money where your mouth is and invest in what are called Notes. We recommend investing a small amount of money in as many notes as possible (often a minimum of $25 per note) in order to minimize your risk.

This is called diversifying your investment.

By diversifying you are ensuring that even if on the off chance that one or two of your loans defaults your overall risk is so minimal that the success of the other notes you are exposed to will allow you to still earn a positive return.

"A truly diversified account has at least 200 equally weighted notes"

– SIMON CUNNINGHAM OF LENDINGMEMO

This would mean that if you are investing $5,000 that you should start with a base of $25 per note.

4) RECEIVE PAYMENTS AND REINVEST

After you make an investment in these notes, you will begin too see payments from your borrowers begin to trickle in. These payments do not occur immediately, as once you committed to put money behind a loan that borrower still needs the loan to be issued in the two weeks it sits on the platform. Once the loan is issued it then still needs to go through the formal process of getting approved by the platform. The borrower then has 30 days after the loan issues before they need to make their first payment.

Once this time period passes however, you will start seeing returns trickle in over time. It is important as we mentioned before to take note of the cash that you have trickling in and your available cash on hand.

From here it's important to take those returns that you are receiving over time and reinvest them back into additional loans. As we mentioned the platforms do not give you any incentive (interest) to hold on to your money, so any money you have just sitting is a wasted opportunity for growth. To get the best bang for your buck you want to make sure you are putting this money to good use by reinvesting it back into loans that you see as valuable, ensuring that you're constantly having your money work harder and smarter for you.

Because of this need to reinvest some people don't like peer to peer lending because they see it as a far more active approach to investing. If in fact you are frustrated with needing to go and reinvest your returns on a frequent basis there is the ability to automate the reinvesting of your loans (even around filters that you have set). We will touch more on the process of automating your investments and the benefits of doing so and several 3rd party outlets that you can leverage to do so.

* * *

MANAGING YOUR INVESTMENT PORTFOLIO

Congratulations you are officially one of the most innovative investors of your time. If by now you have already invested in a variety peer to peer loans, you are at the forefront of an investing revolution.

Now with an account of loans you need to make sure that you are properly managing your account over time. You want to look at all the loans that you are invested in order to track their progress and payment over time.

As we mentioned there is often a long time horizon for a loans life. Just as it is important to keep track of the overall health of your peer to peer account by understanding your return on investment and cash on hand, so to should you check in on the health of the loans you are invested in.

As the payments for loans begin to trickle in it is important that you keep track of each loan's progress as you want to ensure that you are properly reinvesting those return over time.

Stages of a Loan's Life

Healthy Loan: Issued Current Fully Paid

Unhealthy Loan: Issued Current Late Default

While hopefully all of the loans that you invest in will smoothly transition from issued to current to fully paid, it is important to understand what it means when a loan enters into a late or default stage.

As we mentioned these borrowers are human and at times may fall behind on their payments. It is important to understand what happens if this indeed happens and if the borrower is late or defaults on their loans.

UNDERSTANDING LATE LOANS:

Unfortunately, it does sometimes happen that a borrower

will be late on their loans (showing their loan status as late). Typically, there is little reason to worry about this as it is often means that the borrower has run into temporary financial trouble or logistical roadblock (such as changing payments options without updating the loan platform). When these loans go into a "late" stage, the platform will contact the borrower in order to understand what happened with their payment. More often than not these late loans will recover their healthy "current" status in short time.

HOW TO MANAGE DEFAULTS:

However, it is important to note that occasionally these borrowers do default on their loans. Defaulting on a loan means that the individual you lent your money to will not be able to return the loan back in full. In this case you as the investor will not be receiving the full amount of money that you lent out.

"This is the worst part of peer to peer lending"
  – SIMON CUNNINGHAM OF LENDINGMEMO ON DEFAULTS

Fortunately, you as a savvy peer to peer investor have hopefully taken the proper measures to ensure that you do not take a significant financial hit by the borrower's financial troubles. Instead, you intelligently utilized the smart strategy of diversifying your investments not only across a large number of different loans but at a small amount in each, making sure that a single default was not catastrophic on your returns.

Hopefully the rest of your loans are still healthy and being paid back on time when you do experience a default. It can be worrisome at first but the fact of the matter is that almost all peer to peer lenders will experience a default at some point in time. It is important to note that once you when you do experience a default you should look at the health of your current notes and ensure that the rest of them are being paid on time.

"Mistakes are not a problem, not learning from them is"

LEARNING FROM YOUR MISTAKES:

If you find a series of notes that are similarly late and or defaulting it could be an issue as to how your filter is set up and a deeper issue with your overall sorting of loans. It may be important to look back at the descriptions and information about all these loans and see if there are any similarities across the board to learn from moving forward. If there are commonalities between a series of unhealthy notes it may be important to take these shared attributes into account and use them to adjust your loan filters moving forward, developing a more comprehensive strategy around the new the new insights that you've experienced.

In the end, a single default or a series of defaults may prove to educate you on a greater problem that you want to make sure that you avoid down the road in your future investments.

∗ ∗ ∗

YOUR SECRET WEAPON: FILTERING

The secret weapon of the great peer to peer investors is having a well-designed filter or set of filters that they can use to hone out the loans that they want to invest behind. Fortunately for us, both Prosper and Lending Club allow you to benefit from using your own custom filters to sift through the thousands of loans they have available and find the ones that match your risk tolerance. The strength of your filter can greatly determine the quality of the loans you invest in over time. A bad filter could lead to investing in poor loans that in turn default over time, while a good filter could have you investing in far more successful loans in turn experiencing a great return on investment for your account. As such, a great filter can be extremely helpful in your investment process as it streamlines the process for the investor and allows you to hone in on the best loans to invest in early on with tremendous ease. All in all, the process of filtering your loans involve balancing what you deem as healthy risk and unhealthy risk for an investment.

At times we are faced with a risky decision, one that maybe we shouldn't take. But what we have learned over time is to take an internal measurement of the risk at hand and determine whether it's worth our time or not. At times taking a risk does not always need to be a bad thing and can often lead to great things in life.

It's crucial that we are able separate out the times when risk can be healthy and positive in life and when it is bad and detrimental.

Going out the night before final exams is an easy example of an unhealthy risk to take as most of the time it will lead to nothing but harm is your exam performance. On the contrary, putting your name in the ring for that promotion at work, while maybe being seen as a scary risk at the time in, could prove to be a healthy risk in the end to take if you end up getting that promotion.

Throughout our lives we are regularly faced with balancing the healthy and unhealthy risks around us, in essence naturally developing our own filters.

In peer-to-peer lending it is no different. As we are constantly faced with borrowers from all different walks of life it becomes ever more critical that we as investors can easily determine what we see as an unhealthy risk to take in an investment, as well as what we see as a safer or "healthy" risk to take.

This is critical to understanding why it is important that we use filters. As investors in peer-to-peer lending we should understand that there is a direct relationship between the risk we are willing to take as an investor and the return we expect to receive from them. The riskier the investment made on our part (seen through the loan grades) the greater the return we should expect. Filtering allows us to account for certain loans that may not fall exactly in the same risk and reward balance as the rest of them. By understanding what certain factors to look for that can isolate loans that tend to perform better or worse than others, we are able to hone in on opportunities for investment that may have better return potential.

Fortunately for us the world of peer to peer investing is one that is heavily driven by numbers. As such it is far easier to quantify the risk of our investment then whether or not we decide to hit the bars the night before a final exam.

By analyzing the numbers that are directly attached to a given borrower's loan we are able to more closely analyze the exact risks that comprise each borrower's potential returns. The ability to tie values to various attributes of a borrower's profile makes the process of evaluating a loan exponentially easier on us as investors who are able to more quickly able find valuable investment opportunities.

With a vast number of different factors attached to any given loan, we as investors are able to pinpoint exactly which criteria we want to pick out in loans, and eliminate the loans that do not meet our investment expectations or are deemed "too risky" for investment.

"With marketplace and peer-to-peer lending, the difference is transparency"

– SAM HODGES, CO-FOUNDER - FUNDING CIRCLE USA

Fortunately for us all peer to peer lending data is open. This means that the everyday investor can look at the track record of every loan that has been processed through a given platform to gain a better picture as to which criteria have performed best in the past. By leveraging sites such as NSRPlatform.com we are able to look the historically of the different criteria that make up a person's loan and best understand what differentiates one group of loans from another.

Over time we are able to hone in on the criteria that has seen stronger than average returns while similarly isolating certain factors than frequently underperform the typical loan (unhealthy risk). In doing so each investor is able to craft their own unique formula for how they approach the peer to peer lending world, in the end building their ideal filter for loans with a collection of different criteria. By plugging this comprehensive blueprint into the peer to peer platforms we as investors are able to analyze the thousands of loans that are on a platform at a given time and isolate those that meet our standards.

Going to sites like NSRPlatform.com can prove heavily valuable as an investor looking to understand more about where their money is going.

The more time you spend learning the ins and outs of the various criteria that make up these filters, the more that you are able to improve your own filters and in the end reap greater returns on your investments.

Simon Cunningham of LendingMemo explains filtering as a careful balance of good and bad risk. By insuring that we as investors look to avoid taking bad risks while taking on better risks he states that we will be able to maximize our peer to peer returns.

We should have two main criteria in mind one when building out filers: 1) we should look to eliminate the unhealthy risks from our investment and 2) we should look to maximize the healthy risk that we are exposed to.

UNHEALTHY RISK:

Unhealthy risk makes up all those faulty loans that we have

mentioned before: those that default on themselves and don't match up to the risk that we as investors are taking for the return we are receiving.

HEALTHY RISK:

Healthy risk encompasses all of the loans that may be under-priced for the risk that they hold. They in turn are rewarding us with a greater return on investment and give us more return than the risk we are taking. These loans may be historically performing far better than they are priced into the platforms today. As such we should look to invest as much as we can in them.

By maximizing the healthy risk in our investments and minimizing our exposure to unhealthy risk we are giving ourselves as an investor the best shot to experience strong and successful returns the long run.

MINIMIZING THE UNHEALTHY RISK

As we mentioned before, the filters that exist across these platforms allow you to isolate a series of statistics about the borrowers that we can use to minimize our exposure to certain loans.

Imagine that you are an insurance company tasked with

vetting individuals to cover with your health insurance. In any given day you are faced with hundreds of individuals who come to you from all different backgrounds looking for your unique type of insurance coverage. In order to assess the viability of these candidates for your coverage you ask them some basic questions to get to know a little bit more about their background and the specific type of risk that you would be covering them for.

In the end not all the people who come forward would make the best candidate you're your insurance. While one person maybe a healthy mother of five who exercises daily and eats a good meal, you would not be able to discern her from the 55-year-old heavy smoker and adrenaline junkie who likes to skydiving and extreme snowmobiling on a weekly basis. As the insurance company you could not possibly be charging the two the same price for an equal amount of insurance coverage because the two fundamentally have different risks associated with their lifestyles.

The same holds true with peer to peer loans. You need to understand the risk that you are buying into with a given loan before you make your investment. Fortunately, as we've mentioned before these platforms do much of the grunt work for you, pricing out your loans on a given "risk" scale and placing a letter grade on them (With A or AA being the least risk and G or NR carrying the most risk). Each loan grade comes with a corresponding interest rate that the borrowers need to pay given their level of risk. As an investor you can benefit from investing in lower grade (riskier) loans which return a higher interest rate. However, you need to understand that with the increased return comes the increased chances that the borrower on the other side defaults on their loan, thus the worse loan grade.

The lower the letter grade, the riskier the platform thinks that the borrower is to fully return your investment.

Just like the insurance company, you as an investor in the peer to peer space want to understand the important factors that make up your borrower's complete picture. In doing so you are able to perform a more comprehensive assessment of their overall health as a borrower. By looking at quantifiable attributes such as a borrower's credit history, their employment status, or current income, we as investors are able to garner a fuller image of their ability to return our investment.

CREDIT SCORE:

Just as the price of a stock on the stock market fluctuates over time, so too does your borrowers credit history or how reliable they've been in repaying their credit. The higher the credit score, the higher the reliability of the borrower's past ability to repay their loans. This credit score allows us to better understand not only the past history of the borrower but also gauge their ability to pay a loan in the future.

Other Credit Factors to Look at:

- Total Credit Lines
- Open Credit Lines
- Earliest Credit Line
- Delinquencies

CURRENT SITUATION:

One of the more important attributes to look at for a borrower is their current financial situation. Fortunately for us as investors, the lending platform do a great job to ask a variety of detailed questions about the borrower's current financial picture in order to judge their risk and reliability of repaying a loan. Factors such as whether or not they are currently holding a job, how much there are being paid, and even whether they own are rent their home can be key attributes into better understanding the overall risk picture we are looking to invest behind.

Examples of Current Situation Filters:

- Home Ownership
- Annual Income
- Length of Employment (Minimum)

By learning to filter out loans based on the current situation of the borrower you as a lender can make sure that you are making the most out of your effort to reducing unhealthy risk.

PURPOSE OF THE LOAN:

The third key criteria to look at in order to best gauge a borrower's ability to return your investment is to understand the purpose of their loan. While a credit score may show you the borrower's history of being able to repay loans it does not does not give you insight into the types of loans they have been repaying. It is important to understand the risks associated with the various types of loans you could be investing in as they can each have separate levels of risk attached to them. By understanding where your money will be going you can gain a better understanding as to its likelihood of getting repaid in full back to you, the lender. For instance, a loan to start someone's business may have historically have a higher default rate than one that is going to help someone refinance their credit card debt, or go toward a home improvement. As such you need to understand the factors that can be attributed to riskier loans so as to ensure you are not investing in a loan that could pose a greater risk then potentially safer ones that are paying out the same interest rate.

Examples of Loan Purposes:

- Refinancing Credit Card
- Consolidating Debt
- Medical Expenses
- Business Loan
- Home Improvement Project
- Home Down Payment

INQUIRY HISTORY:

Another important criteria to look at when filtering through potential loans is the inquiry history of the borrower. The inquiry history on the borrower (often narrowed down to the past six months) is the number of hard inquiries the borrower has in their credit history. Often, borrowers with a lower inquiry history are safer investments then their counterparts with higher inquiries. As a result, isolating for those with no inquiries can prove to be a valuable component of any successful filter.

REDLINING:

We all know that there each state in the United States has its own unique attributes. However, would you have guesses that there would be a difference in peer to peer returns between various states? It turns out that data proves that the return you receive on your peer to peer investment can be impacted by the state in which you make your loan. Curious what the worst state for loans are? The top four states to avoid are Florida, Nevada, California, and Arizona. Whether it is their frenzied culture or the history of poor housing markets, these states hold the lowest rate of return for investors and should be avoided when filtering your loans.

* * *

MAXIMIZING HEALTHY RISK

After you filter out for a variety of unhealthy risk in the loans, it is important to look to amplify the healthy risk that you as an investor can be exposed to through your loans. Taking on healthy risk means that you may be able to experience greater returns than the risk you could be taking in other loans. By isolating out certain factors that are deemed more positive attributes for a loan, thus making them more likely to be paid back you as an investor can look to benefit from potentially greater returns with reduced risk then loans of a similar grade.

Throughout peer to peer lending, some loans are riskier than others and some are more likely to get paid back than others. The same holds true in that some attributes of borrowers can make them are far safer bet than others. To account for this these platforms, tag a riskier loan grade on those loans that are less likely to get repaid.

Loan Grades

Safer		Prosper		Lending Club	Lower Return
	AA	6-8%	A	6-8%	
	A	9-11%	B	9-12%	
	B	12-14%	C	13-15%	
	C	15-18%	D	16-18%	
	D	19-22%	E	19-22%	
	E	23-28%	F	23-25%	
Riskier	HR	29-30%	G	26%	Higher Return

As the loan grade goes from better to worse so too does the interest rate that the borrower pays and that the lender receives goes up. Some investors find it extremely valuable to diversify their portfolio across not only the safest loans, return lower yields, but to occasionally invest in riskier loans that can return larger yields back to the lender. By mixing in riskier loans with safer, more typical loans you as an investor are able to increase your chances of increasing your chances for a higher return thus generating a stronger return on investment.

For example, while an "A" loan on lending club may only yield between 6-9%, by mixing in several "D" loans that return 17-20% could be a good helpful for your overall portfolio, assuming that you are evenly diversified across a variety of loans.

Finding riskier, higher grade loans, thus can be helpful in reaching stronger returns in the end so long as you filter these with similar criteria that you developed in the past.

In the end, it all depends on your risk tolerance. While some people find it valuable to mix in riskier loans that can reach higher in the end there are more than enough people on these platforms who are comfortable investing only in the lowest risk and highest grade loans (the A's and B's) As these loans are least likely to fail and as such lock or are more likely to lock in a more than reasonable consistent 5-7% return on investment. On top of this there is plenty of evidence to suggest that given another downturn in the market and the country's economy that these "safer" loans will be the ones that are least susceptible to impact and defaulting.

For younger people such as myself and others we see far more long term value in taking a riskier approach to investing. As I am not nearing the age of retirement anytime soon, diversifying into several riskier loans that I have filtered out alongside with some safer options is fine as I am increasing my chances of stronger returns.

EXAMPLE FILTERS TO USE

Example Beginner Filter:

Grade: A, B, C
Inquiries in the last 6 months = 0
Loan Purpose: Exclude Business Loans
States Excluded: Arizona, Nevada, Florida, California
Annual Income: Over $70,000

Example High Return Filter to Use:

Below is Peter Renton of LendAcademy and LendIt's Simple
High Return Filter Strategy:
Grade: C, D, E
Inquiries in the last 6 months = 0
Loan Purpose: Debt Reconsolidation, Credit Card Refinance
Optional: Home Ownership: Mortgage or Own
Optional: Annual Income over $45,000

* * *

Overall the goal of using filters should be to effectively sift
through loans and reduce as much of the unhealthy risk that
you as an investor are exposed to, while increasing the healthy
risk in your portfolio.

While finding the exact type of loan to invest in is no perfect
science, developing your filters is far more of a creative skill
than a pure science. As you spend more time with platforms
your ability to develop filters that you deem most appropriate
for your risk tolerance will increase with it.

Regardless of the comprehensive filters that some investors use,
there are still plenty of individuals on these platforms who do
not bother to filter through loans and merely invest directly
into the loans that they see. These investors still experience

the strong returns on the peer to peer platforms, but more consistently in the range of 5-7%. My belief is that while you can achieve successful returns without using filter, doing so will only enhance your opportunities for return. The more that you are able to hone in your filtering skills and develop a concrete and effective strategy to find loans, the greater the chances you have of beating out your peers and reaching returns of 9% and greater.

* * *

DIVERSIFICATION, RISKS & AUTOMATING INVESTMENTS
DIVERSIFICATION

While filtering can help you figure out the loans that you want to invest in by eliminating the unhealthy risk and finding those with healthy risk, in the end the real game changer in ensuring a strong lasting return in your portfolio is properly diversifying. Far too often you hear about negative reactions to peer to peer lending from individuals who lost money on a platform. This is often because these investors spread their money across too few loans.

Take this example:

Investor A and B both have $1000 to invest in peer to peer loans. Investor A decided they do not need to diversify their investment and decide to invest their $1000 across 10 loans with $100 being placed in each. Investor B is a savvier investor and decides to invest their $1000 across 40 different loans with $25 in each. When both investors experience a default on one of their loans Investor A (with 10 loans) is furious at the peer to peer marketplace. This is because his single default on a loan made up for 10% of his entire portfolio (1 out of 10 loans). Investor B on their other hand, while disappointed in their loss understands that their diversified portfolio (2.5% in each loan) will most likely make up for their losses.

If you only invest across ten loans and one of them defaults, the other nine loans need to perform far harder than the typical loan to make up for that loss and minimize the blow to your portfolio. As a result, it is crucial that you make sure that you are investing your portfolio across as many loans as possible.

While experts vary of the minimum number of loans you should have to properly diversify we recommend that you invest across is 200+ loans. At a minimum investment of $25, this $5000 minimum investment ensures that your historical odds of positive return are nearly 100%.

The reason for this boils down to the fact that the more notes you are invested in the less you are impacted by one if it defaults.

We as investors need to understand, all of these borrowers are human and face their own challenges. As such, we need to come to the understanding that some of the loans that we are invested in may default. Minimizing the impact that one of these loans has on our portfolio is key. As such, we should ensure that not only are we investing in as many loans we can, on the same note that no one or few loans has a far greater amount than others invested in them.

By evenly investing in $25 or $50 increments across all of our two hundred plus loans we are ensuring that we're dispersing the risk and the blow that could be received by a bad blow. More specifically we are reducing the volatility that we as an investor would experience if conditions go south. By not an eliminating the risk of these loans but reducing the impact a single one would have we are ensuring the long-term success of our peer to peer investment portfolio.

We can see this relationship firsthand in the lending club return by portfolio size. With each additional loan, we see the chances for negative return decreasing with some of these platforms reaching near zero for investors who have evenly diversified across 200+ loans.

While we cannot promise positive success, the closest thing that we can do to ensure the healthiest and strongest performance in our peer to peer investments is by ensuring that you as an investor diversify as best you can.

While we cannot ensure that all of our loans will be successful and reap positive returns in the end, the best we can do is ensure that we are doing all that we can to prevent our downside. By evenly diversifying in 200+ loans of an even amount, we are ensuring that we maximize our exposure to positive returns and minimize the hit that can be had if any one loan defaults. By diversifying across a variety of different factors and ensuring that we are supposed to an even level of risk across the board, we as a peer to peer investor are maximizing our opportunity for success.

RISKS

With any investment it is important to understand the risk associated with investing. Peer to Peer lending in particular has a unique set of risks to keep in mind. With it being such a new industry it is ever more important to understand exactly what you are getting involved with as an investor.

Undoubtedly you as an investor are going to experience defaults on some of the loans you invest in. If you are smart to diversify properly as have previously mentioned your account should still reap the many tremendous returns that a peer to peer portfolio can have.

Nonetheless there are still negative variety of negative factors that could negatively affect your portfolio and that you as an investor should understand.

Risks to Peer to Peer Lending:

- Recession
- Interest Rates
- Default Risk
- Unemployment
- Liquidity Risk
- Regulation
- Platform Bankruptcy

As the industry as a whole has not fully weathered a recession or rising unemployment it will be interesting to see exactly how those trends impact loan repayments. With major players in the space being well-established companies we should feel a certain level of certainty of the quality of the loans being given. Nonetheless, these risks should be taken into account before anyone makes an investment in the on a peer to peer platform.

RESEARCH

With the data on peer to peer lending being open to the masses, the ability to understand the historical performance of various loans is one of the critical advantages to the space. Thus, as a new investor you are going to want to answer several questions before you enter into the world of peer to peer lending:

- How much should I invest?
- What is my time horizon for investing?

What is my risk tolerance (Conservative vs. Aggressive?)

Fortunately for us as investors, there are a variety of different resources across the Internet to better understand your answers to these questions. Through using a platform such as NSRPlatform.com we are able to look closely at the historical analytics behind any specific filter to better understand how your investment objectives align with these loans historical performance.

AUTOMATING YOUR INVESTMENT

Although we went into great depth as to how you can filter through the thousands of loans on a platform, if you prefer to take a more passive approach there are a variety of solutions available to you. As the industry has developed both platforms and third party entities have crafted unique ways of automating your investment portfolio. Both Lending Club as well as Prosper have automatic tools that you can easily implement (even using your existing filters) if your account is above a certain threshold.

Similarly, there are a variety of third party players who have entered into the space. These companies allow you to automate your peer to peer investing portfolio given your investment objectives and risk tolerance, even allowing you to easily diversify across multiple platforms. By ensuring that your investments are being professionally managed and funds are reinvested as they come in, these emerging players are breaking down many of the difficulties that have existed in peer to peer lending.

Several of these peer to peer investment managers are:

- NSR Invest
- BlueVestment
- LendingRobot
- PeerCube

In the end it is up to you as an investor as to how you want to approach the peer to peer lending space. There are a variety of different methods to take in entering into the space but all in all, it is a unique opportunity to differentiate your portfolio away from other typical investments.

FIVE

EQUITY CROWDFUNDING

"Making entrepreneurship more inclusive isn't just a moral imperative, it's an economic one."

- STEVE CASE, CO-FOUNDER OF AOL

Imagine that you are flipping through a sleek new online investment platform. Instead of flipping through stocks on the New York Stock Exchange or the NASDAQ, in front of you are hundreds of private companies reaching out to find investors. As you flip from listing to listing one company catches your attention. Their listing claims "affordable benefits for your company in minutes".

Sounds interesting. You decide to look closer at the company.

It looks like there are trying to help streamline the payroll and benefits process for companies. You have heard countless from a friend struggling to manage these issues in their own company so you can begin to relate to the problem. You are still not entirely sure what makes this company unique so you do some more research, checking out the founding team and what their product really is.

The founders look like they are for real (with backgrounds in the industry) and the business seems like it is really on to something (having 15 clients and over 70 already on a waitlist). The company has even already raised $372,000 from 10 high profile investors.

Heck, why not. You decide to invest. At a company valuation of $9 million, you decide to invest $500 (enough skin in the game to make a difference, but won't kill you).

As the months after making your investment pass, you keep tabs on the company, following it in the news and seeing how things are going. So far what you have been hearing has been great, it looks like they are growing with speed and the media is catching on.

Less than a year after you invested the company announces that they have raised an additional $15 million at a valuation of $70 million. The investment your made is already worth more than 7 times what you put it into the company at and the company looks like it is still growing strong. Less than six months after that fundraising round, the company raised another round at a valuation of $500 million. But it does not stop there. Less than two years after your original investment the company raises another $500 million at a valuation of $4.5 billion!

Meet Zenefits.

Zenefits is one of the great early success stories of equity crowdfunding, having raised $50,000 on the equity crowdfunding platform WeFunder.

Had you invested $500 in Zenefits when you first came across it on WeFunder, your investment would be worth $250,000 (a 500x return)!

Welcome to the world of startup investing, where you can get in on the ground floor of companies that are capable of experiencing growth far quicker than you could ever imagine. While it is certainly a risky undertaking, the opportunity to invest in the visionaries are tomorrow can prove limitless.

* * *

Welcome to the world of equity crowdfunding!

Imagine being able to directly invest in the next big fast food franchise, hot new travel app or local clean energy start-up with as little as $100. And imagine having an idea for a new company and raising $1 million from friends as well as people you don't know, yet who believe in your vision.

While peer-to-peer lending had to do with the lending of money to individuals, equity crowdfunding uses a similar concept except to provide equity capital for a business. Instead of lending money to an individual to be paid out over a period of time with a defined return, equity crowdfunding allows you to invest directly into a business that requires capital to fund growth and acquire additional resources.

Virtually, since its inception, our country has been a nation of small business and entrepreneurs. Whether it is the local family owned deli, the local barber, or the mom and pop ice cream shop, the small towns of America have long relied upon the ability for small business to exist. In the past if these businesses want to look to grow and expand they would often need to go to a bank to request a business loan that they would pay back over time. The business would then use this loan to help finance its growth.

Today we are living in one of the greatest entrepreneurial revolutions that history has ever seen. But it is not the expanding of small businesses such as our local deli and ice cream shops that are fueling this next great economic surge. Instead we have entered a transformational age powered by technology. When two college students in a dorm room can put their blood sweat and tears a new idea into an idea and generate the next billion-dollar business, we see the true power of our digital age. The integration of internet and software in our day to day lives has served as "rocket fuel" for the next generation of value creation.

However, just like these mom and pop businesses require capital to grow their store or expand their business, oftentimes these software and internet companies require investment to expand their business.

This is where venture capitalists typically come into the picture. These larger groups of institutional investors go out and look to find young entrepreneurial firms that hope to develop the next big idea. By uncovering what they believe will be the next great business, venture firms provide the growth capital that funds many start-ups and the dreams of their founding entrepreneurs. These investors provide capital and invest their money alongside the founders, buying a piece of equity in the overall company.

Example: Imagine being able to have invested $100 in FaceBook when it had only been valued at $5,000,000 in 2004. Today FaceBook is publicly traded and has a market cap of over $333 *billion. Had you invested $100 in 2004 your investment would now be worth over $6,650,000 (a 66,600 times return!).*

As the company grows over time, so too does the value of the firm's equity. Venture investors have purchased an equity interest in the dreams and aspirations of the founding entrepreneurs and will join them on their journey to create value and generate a return for their investors.

This traditionally exclusive world of venture capital is being transformed by the emergence of technology enabled platforms that link networks of individuals with investment opportunities. Welcome to the world of crowdfunding. Rewards-based crowdfunding platforms such as Kickstarter or Indiegogo started the movement of the "crowd" allowing people to put small chunks of money to support ideas they saw as being the next great product or service. These early crowdfunding platforms were limited in their sophistication. Initially, the only legal method of reward that businesses who went out to raise support could give to these donors was anything non-monetary. Whether it is a T-shirt, a tweet, or the early adoption of a product, the only incentive that these supporters could have received for their support of the business was non-cash related.

THE JOBS ACT

In 2012, President Obama signed The Jumpstart Our Business

Startups (JOBS) Act. The Acts passing initiated a domino effect that has led to the world of equity crowdfunding as we know it today. The passing of the JOBS Act allowed for any business that wanted to go out and raise money publicly from individual investors to do so. Where once only big investment groups (and venture firms) could invest directly into a private company, now individuals of all kinds were able to invest their hard earned money directly into the businesses.

I believe that the JOBS Act will ultimately prove to be the catalyst driving a tremendous wave of innovation that will reshape the business world. As more and more entrepreneurs have ready access to the capital to finance their ideas and grow their businesses thru leveraging crowd sourced investment, we will likely see a significant amount of value creation spread across our country.

BENEFITS OF EQUITY VS. REWARDS-BASED CROWDFUNDING

When explaining the idea of equity crowdfunding to someone, the first response is often "Isn't that just like Kickstarter?" While Kickstarter is a great example of the power of crowd-funding, it is important to understand the differences that exist between rewards-based crowdfunding platform and equity-based crowdfunding.

On reward-based crowdfunding platforms, such as Kickstarter, an individual company is able to go out and post their product, often coming up with an innovative promotional video to raise its profile to the public and solicit funds from anyone who comes across the site. However, when these individuals do come forward and commit their money to the project, by law the only reward that these companies are able to give their supporters are non-cash incentives. As a result, you see t-shirts, tweets, and access to early product offerings pushed through these platforms in an effort to best incentivize individuals to donate to their campaigns. Donate being the key word. These are not investments.

On the other side is equity crowdfunding. As its name suggests, equity crowdfunding allows individuals to invest directly in the equity (ownership) of these companies. By allowing you to "put your money where your mouth is" you as an investor are able to buy an actual piece of equity in the company. The value of your investment can grow or shrink over time based on the fortunes of the company. Fortunately, in this case your success is directly tied to that of the company and you're not simply left with an extra t-shirt sitting in your drawer or an old prototype.

I believe that we are at the cusp of a new wave of innovation, and equity crowdfunding's emergence onto the investing scene is about to provide a seismic shift in how companies interact with their investors and will open up a new world of value creation.

* * *

HOW DOES IT WORK?

HOW IT WORKS ON TV

Many of us are familiar with the popular investing TV show Shark Tank. In it we are able to see a panel of experienced entrepreneurs with money to invest hear the next great ideas of tomorrow. By cycling entrepreneurs across through their studio to pitch their business these "sharks" are able to buy into a stake of the company and provide their expertise to help grow it over time. Unfortunately, we often see these "sharks" looking to bite off more than the entrepreneur was hoping for, often investing in far more of the company for far less of a valuation then the business owner had hoped for.

HOW STARTUP INVESTING ACTUALLY WORKS

A pair of innovative entrepreneurs come together to develop the next great business. As they spend hundreds of hours in their home office flushing through the details of the business and begin the hard work of building the business from the ground up, they realize that they are not generating enough money to grow the business like they want. Unfortunately for them their company does not have enough physical collateral to go and request a loan, as the bank could not be sure that these two would ever be able to fully repay the money that they were requesting. As a result, the founders of the company go out to a panel of venture capitalists with their great idea. These entrepreneurs pitch what they believe is the future success of their business to venture capitalists who have the money to invest. In the end, the venture capitalists either take a pass or agree to buy a piece of the company (equity) for a given price.

By buying a piece of the company the venture capitalists are able to buy a seat alongside these entrepreneurs as they grow their business. If this current million dollar company becomes a billion dollar company the possibilities for return for the venture capitalists are truly exponential.

* * *

There are two main ways to invest in early-stage startups. You can either invest in a priced equity round or you can invest in what are called "convertible securities". As a future early stage investor, it is important to understand what makes each unique:

Priced Equity Round: Buying into a company through a priced equity round means that you are buying into a piece (shares) of a company at a fixed price (valuation). You know exactly how many shares of the company you are buying into because the valuation for the company is already set.

Convertible Securities: The more common method of investing in early stage companies, convertible securities allow you to invest a certain amount of money into a company at a valuation that will be determined at a later date. This ensures that you as an investor are not placing too high of a burden on the current valuation of a company that has yet to mature its business model. Your investment will "convert" into equity when the company performs its next round of investment at a more concrete valuation.

The concept of equity crowdfunding is pretty simple. Instead of startups going to a team of profit-hungry venture capitalists to raise their money, they instead open up ownership in their business to the investing public. In a similar fashion that a borrower goes to a peer-to-peer platform to raise their loans money from the crowd, these businesses look to connect with equity crowdfunding platforms to perform their investment round online.

A company looking to raise money first reaches out to a platform and applies to be listed on their site to raise money. These equity crowdfunding platforms then perform their own vetting of these companies (due diligence) to better understand the viability of each individual business. The process of getting onto a competitive crowdfunding site is fairly comprehensive with the most successful platforms accepting less than 0.5% of those who apply.

Just as any venture capitalist wants to understand the risks and rewards of the business they are potentially investing in, these platforms want to make sure that they are offering viable investment opportunities to their investor community. As a result, they perform a similar level of due diligence that any potential venture capital would undertake when looking at an investment opportunity. By better understanding the various attributes that make up the business, whether the founding team, the market they are entering, the value proposition, or the health of their finances, these platforms are able best vet potential investment opportunities before they offer them to their users.

Once a business is approved to be listed on a platform, a valuation is determined for the company and the business states a certain level of equity or investment that are looking to open up to the crowd. Just like on Kickstarter, these companies have a set time period in which their equity offering is open to the public. Typically, there will be a minimum amount of investment required for any equity to be transacted. This ensures that no one investor is left with an equity stake in an underfunded company.

However, unlike reward-based crowdfunding, there is a cap to the potential money that a company can raise as it cannot give an unlimited amount of equity away. Once the equity offering closes, the money is then transferred to the business (minus a small fee for the platform) and the equity to the investors.

As a potential investor, you will be the person going to these platforms and searching through the various opportunities listed in hopes of finding your next great startup investment. In order to do this, you first need to go onto one of the various equity crowdfunding platforms, whether it is WeFunder, SeedInvest, Fundable, or one of countless others, and submit an application to become an Investor. (*Know that some platforms still restrict access to accredited investors: those with a net worth over $1 Million or an annual income over $200,000*) Once you open an account on a platform you are then able to freely browse through the current listings and discover companies actively seeking money. This is where the equity crowdfunding process gets both exciting but also confusing as there are so many different opportunities to invest.

How can you as an investor possibly know which businesses to put your money behind?

The fact of the matter is that no one knows whether or not a business will be successful in the end. Oftentimes the role of a venture capitalist investing in early stage companies is more art than science.

Every venture capitalist has different criteria for what they look for in judging a potential investment. Over time, as you gain more experience in investing in early stage companies so will you be able to better hone in on the exact attributes that you look for in a potential investment. Whether you want to focus on a single industry or invest only in a certain business model, you will learn to perform your own unique due diligence, properly vetting ideas as you see fit.

In the end, these equity crowdfunding platforms have made it easier than ever for the everyday investor to unlock the unique opportunity of investing in in early stage companies. As you spend more time with these platforms and increase your venture capital abilities you will be able to more quickly judge which ideas are fundamentally flawed from those ideas which may have the potential to grow.

The best advice that I can share with you is to start slow and small when making your first investments. Never invest more than you can afford to lose as there is no promise of seeing a return in any sort of early stage investment. The more time that you spend understanding the platforms, the more comfortable you will get in understanding the ins and outs of what makes each investment tick. Many platforms allow you make investments as low as $100 and I recommend that you, especially early on, spread your total investment amount across as many potential startups as possible.

The next sections will provide an overview on some of the key features that many investors in the past have used to gauge possible investment opportunities and will hopefully help set you off on the road becoming the next great early stage investor.

* * *

WHAT MAKES STARTUP INVESTING DIFFERENT?

Being able to invest in the next great idea and support the next great startup or growth company is one of the most unique opportunities that you could have as an investor. As an investor, it is important to understand that investing in a startup is not the same as investing in a public market stock such as Facebook or Apple. Investing in these publicly traded stocks have a variety of differences than had you invested in an early round of a private company such as AirBnb or Uber. When beginning to look at investing in early stage private companies it is important to understand the key pieces that separate them from their pubic counterparts.

Timelines: While a stock in Apple or Facebook could in theory be bought today and sold for a profit tomorrow, the same cannot be said for investing in a private company. Most early stage investments need to be held for 5-7 years before the investor is able to receive a return. As a result, it is important to understand how long your money is going to be invested before committing to anything.

Selling Stock: When a company is publicly traded on the stock market it's price changes almost constantly and you as an investor have the ability to buy and sell a share at almost any time. As of right now there is unfortunately no secondary market for shares of private companies. This means that you as an investor in an early stage company need to wait for either an acquisition, IPO, or additional round of funding before being able to sell your shares.

Returns: While you could, in theory, buy a public stock on Monday and sell it on Tuesday for a profit, your timeline for return on a public company is far longer. As we mentioned it typically requires 5-7 years before you as an investor will be able to see any return on your investment. While you rarely see massive price changes in a public company, the benefit of investing in an early stage private company is that you open yourself to far greater return possibilities. With your investment timeline stretched out over 5-7 years you often see the value of your investment either going completely to zero or being worth far more than it was originally worth. As an investor it is important to understand how your range of returns will vary in a private investment versus a publicly traded one.

THE REWARDS OF STARTUP INVESTING

While startup investing is far different from investing in a large public company, there are countless rewards for entering into this dynamic and growing ecosystem and helping the next great ideas get launched off the ground.

Support The Entrepreneurial Community: By investing early in a startup you are helping the entrepreneurs of tomorrow push their ideas forward and grow the greater entrepreneurial community at large. This push only further encourages more and more people to enter into it and fosters the next wave of great ideas. The psychic reward of helping an entrepreneur realize her dream can be quite rewarding in itself.

Potentially Great Returns: Investing in a startup means that you're buying into a small piece of a potentially growing company. As a result, your opportunity of gaining larger returns are far greater than you might see in buying a typical stock in the public markets. The small chance of a great upside can be enough times to drive even the most frugal investors to the startup investing world.

Overall Diversification: By adding the investment a small piece of a potentially much larger business later on in your overall investment you are adding a unique level of risk to your portfolio.

* * *

PLANNING YOUR INVESTMENT STRATEGY

The ability to invest in early stage companies offers a variety of exciting opportunities for you as an investor to reap the tremendous benefits that in the past were closed off to venture capitalists. However just like the successful venture capitalists of the world do, it is important to plan for your portfolio of start-ups before you blindly start investing in early stage companies.

SETTING AN INVESTMENT STRATEGY

The most successful venture capitalists of the world often have an overall strategy guiding their investment decisions. This allows them to make more informed and more successful decisions on the companies that they choose to put their money behind. In the end, honing in on certain factors and developing your own personal "venture capital brand" allows you to improve your overall abilities to invest, making the process all the more enjoyable.

Some typical criteria that venture capitalists will think about in launching a fund are: stage of company that they will invest in, market sector, geography, business models, investment size, and number of investments. Every venture capital has a different approach to these six criteria making each unique in their approach to investing. Whether you are a $1-million-dollar fund or a $10 million you need to understand your unique approach to your investments.

STAGE OF COMPANY

It is important to understand what stage of a business you want to focus your investments on. Is it seed stage, where the company may have just have an idea and little market traction? Early stage, where there is some proof of concept, but not a strong record of financials behind it? Or later, growth stage, where they have shown a greater level of success and proven market and are looking to grow to the next level?

MARKET SECTOR

It is similarly important to understand what industries you want to start investing behind. Often this can be the result of our own past experience and our ability to better understand the ins and outs of an industry. Successful venture capitalists often invest in industries that they themselves had a history in and can better understand. By investing in industries that you have a unique knowledge in, you are better able to understand the unique ins and out that will make the business competitive in the future. By focusing in on a sector and more continuously following it, you give yourself the advantage of better understanding where unique opportunities will be in the sector down the road, and a leg up for future opportunities.

GEOGRAPHY

Understanding geographically where you want to focus your

investments can prove helpful. As different markets and entrepreneurial "hubs" can have different success rates and the ability to leverage additional resources, it is helpful to understand how a company's location can affect it as an investment.

BUSINESS MODELS

Understanding the business models that you hope to invest in will allow you as an investor to more quickly analyze unique Investment opportunities as they come up. Typically venture capitalists will have expertise in certain business models so that they understand exactly how a company will be able to leverage it and provide a strategic advantage as they grow. Whether it is focusing on SaaS (software as a service) companies, marketplaces, consumer, or eCommerce, understanding what models you want to target can be a key building block for your overall investment strategy.

INVESTMENT SIZE

The size of the investments you make will largely be driven off of the total amount of money you want to invest in startups. As you do not want to "put all your eggs in one basket" it is important to space out the size of your investments across number of different companies. Experts recommend investing in no less than 10 companies, so take this into account as you begin to decide how much money you want to put into start investments.

A Piece of Advice: Make sure that you have capital ready to invest when you begin looking through investments. The last thing that you want to do is spend hours diving through business models and understanding investment opportunities only to find that you don't have the money you want to invest easily available.

NUMBER OF INVESTMENTS

As startup investing is highly risky, you want to make sure that you spread your risk across a number of different investments. This ensures that even if one or a few of your investments fail, you will still have the opportunity to see your money back and potentially return a profit. *"Don't put all your eggs in one basket"*.

* * *

ACCOUNTING FOR RISK

Startup investments are some of most risky investments that you as an investor can make. With failure rates being high and the time horizon for your return on investment typically stretching 5 to 7 years, it is important to understand the risk that you as an investor are undertaking before you put invest any of your money.

There are several factors you should take into before you enter the exciting world of equity crowdfunding.

OVERALL ALLOCATION

Experts recommend not investing more than 5-10% of your overall portfolio on startup investments. By balancing some more traditional investment opportunities with your riskier startup investments you allow yourself to not risk all of your life savings on the chances of hitting the next billion-dollar company. While still being able to reap the tremendous rewards if one of your investments does exceedingly well, you making sure that you are covering the overall safety of your investments.

DIVERSIFICATION

As with peer-to-peer loans you want to make sure that no one startup will make or break your entire investment strategy. It is important to invest across a minimum of at least 10-15 startups to make sure that you can reap the rewards if one is successful, but while not being exposed if one fails. Typically venture capital funds make a majority of their returns off of one or two "home run" investments. While several of their investments will fail, and some will break even. It is often the one or few investments that are able to return 5-10+ times the original investment that make up for the shortcomings of the rest.

INVESTMENT TIMELINE

It is important to understand that you will not be able to get your investment back immediately. Do not invest any money that you will need access to in the short term. As it the typical startup investment horizon is 5 to 7 years your money will be locked up in a private company for the foreseeable future.

* * *

DOING YOUR HOMEWORK – PART I: UNDERSTANDING THE COMPANY

Congratulations!

By now I hope that you are well on your way to becoming the next great startup investor. With a strategy now in place for how your personal "VC Fund" aligns with your own goals and objectives, now comes the exciting time to start looking for investments.

UNDERSTANDING THE PLATFORMS

To start, it's important to understand the platform that you to make your investments. As no two platforms are the same it is important to understand what makes each of the various equity crowdfunding options unique. While some may focus only on emerging consumer goods and others on software, it is important to keep in mind how you want to position your investments when deciding what platforms to use. As these platforms are constantly updating their listings, it is important to check their investment opportunities on a regular basis.

It is similarly important to understand the quality of the platform that you are using to invest. As these platforms will vet the deals that they list in-house, it is important to understand the quality of deals that each platform will release to the public. Each platform will hold different standards for what they deem as a quality investment opportunity and can serve as a key initial funnel for understanding investment opportunities.

UNDERSTANDING THE INVESTMENT

Now that you found a platform that you want to invest in and have been searching through their opportunities for some time, you come across a startup that you think could be an interesting to invest in.

But how can you do your own research to make sure that you can trust your money is going toward a reliable investment?

As we mentioned, VC funds perform what's called "due diligence" or in-house research to vet the companies, their business models, and the viability of them as future investments.

Just as these platforms have done an initial vetting of the businesses that come to them, the due diligence process for VC funds, separate out those who are successful from those who face continuing losses.

Each venture capitalist has a different approach as to what they look for in a particular company. What follows is a common overarching approach that you can use to begin to better understand the ins and outs of your potential investment opportunity and its opportunity for success down the road.

DOING YOUR HOMEWORK –
UNDERSTANDING THE COMPANY

Overall, the process of performing proper due diligence on a company involves several stages. With diving deeper in researching the company, you as the investor are better able to uncover pieces of the overall puzzle and assess the true investment potential. Think of the due diligence process as a funnel for you as an investor. While 100 ideas may come forward initially, as you perform each part of the due diligence process and develop a more unique understanding for how the business operates, you begin to eliminate ideas that are flawed.

A venture capital firm may have a hundred businesses go through its due diligence funnel, but only end up with one viable investment opportunity. Having a thorough understanding of exactly what you look for and developing your expertise over time will help you to hone in on exactly which businesses you could find long-term value investing behind.

Fortunately for us, we do not need to reinvent the wheel in terms of due diligence. There are a variety of resources out there that state a broad multi-step process for understanding an investment. As a result, we as investors in equity crowdfunding can start with a more general understanding of the process, and develop our own unique process and expertise over time.

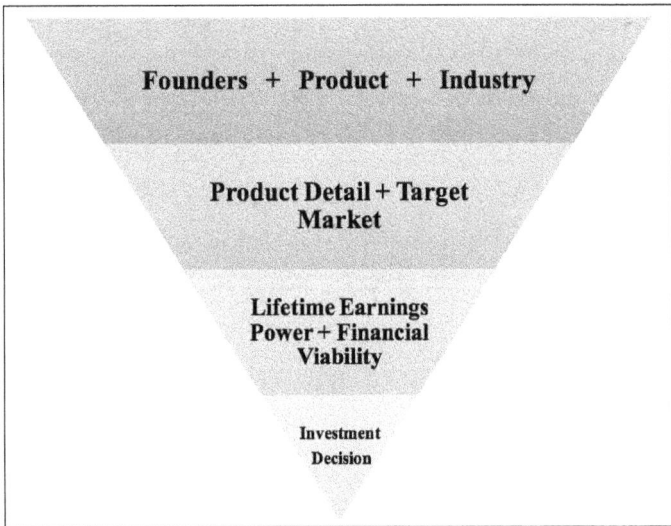

Founders + Product + Industry

Product Detail + Target Market

Lifetime Earnings Power + Financial Viability

Investment Decision

The four step funnel that MicroVentures (a prominent equity crowdfunding site) lists here provides a with a unique glimpse into the unique due diligence process. As they progress from stages one to two to three, finally resulting in an investment decision in stage four. The deeper due diligence progression over time allows you as an investor to more thoroughly understand business by eliminating those with clearest faults early on. By eliminating out the most obvious faults in a business early on, you as a potential investor can make sure that you are not wasting your time looking at more detailed observations of a fundamentally flawed business.

PART I: THE FOUNDING TEAM, PRODUCT, INDUSTRY (AND VALUE PROPOSITION)

The first step in our due diligence process covers some of the highest level parts of a given business. By looking at a business's founding team, its product, its industry, and its value proposition, we as an investor are better able to gauge an overall picture for how this company will differentiate itself from the pack. While we won't be able to understand the full business profile for a company by looking at these attributes, we can start to build a more general idea for it's future down the road.

THE FOUNDING TEAM

Having a strong founding team is crucial for any successful investment. A strong founding team will serve as the building blocks for consistent and strong growth over time. As such it is important to do a deep vetting as to exactly who comprises your potential investment's founding team.

By looking at factors such as their history, overall ability, versatility and how well they have executed in the past, you as an investor can better gauge how they will be able to flow with the bumps and bruises that come with building a startup company.

PRODUCT OR SERVICE

This first take on the company will look at the product from a higher level, understanding exactly where it positions itself and the basic structure of where they as a company see it differentiating in the marketplace. It is important to understand what you are dealing with from a product standpoint. While having a great founding team and entering into a strong industry are pivotal for a startup's success, without a strong product to tie it all together, the prospects for long-term viability are tough. Therefore, it is important to find a product who's vision you can buy into and one that you think can make an impact and scale down the road.

INDUSTRY

As you grow in your ability to invest in startups, it will be important to look at industry trends and find unique opportunities in growing industries as there will be more opportunity for growth industries that are growing in size in value then those are attracting. It is important to look and the ins and outs of the industry that a company is in as it is important you understand the competitive landscape and customer base that your investment will have to deal with.

VALUE PROPOSITION

Understanding a company's value proposition will allow you to understand the deeper roots that make a company unique. While having a strong founding team and market to tackle are important, a company's value proposition will serve is got a true blueprint for your product moving forward. It articulates exactly why you are doing what you do as a business.

"People don't buy what you do; they buy why you do it. And what you do simply proves what you believe"

- SIMON SINEK

I personally believe that a business driven by a strong value proposition is far more likely to succeed than one without one. It is what separates the Apple's of the world from the Microsoft's and can serve as a vital component for long term success.

PART II: PRODUCT DETAIL AND PRODUCT MARKET

Once you have successfully dug through part one of the due diligence process it is time to look at your business with a slightly narrower focus. By targeting product, a detail and product market we are better able to understand exactly where this business can create value in the world.

PRODUCT DETAIL

While our first look at the business's product looked more at the overall product, our dive into product detail will allow us to more completely understand the ins and out of what make the product tick. It will allow us to understand exactly what the faults of the product are and where barriers to growth stand, ultimately best understanding it's long term prospects.

PRODUCT MARKET

By looking at a product's market we are better able to understand exactly where it fits in the overall landscape of its market. By understanding if a product is entering into a large market that is already populated with a variety of competitors, or if it is entering into one with little or no competition, we are better able to understand the challenges that the company will face over time.

PART III: A CLOSER LOOK AT FINANCIALS

The third step in our due diligence funnel is to look more deeply at the financials of the business. By understanding exactly how the company will earn money and grow over time, we will better understand the chances that our investment will be worth more a year from now than it is today.

LIFETIME EARNINGS POWER

A company's lifetime earnings power represents its ability to generate revenue over its lifespan. By understanding exactly how much money it will generate we are best able to gauge how much money we may be putting in today compared to how much money the companies could potentially be generating down the road.

FINANCIAL VIABILITY

It is important to understand the various costs associated with business you are looking at. By understanding exactly what costs the company needs to deal with on a day to day basis, we are best able to understand the financial viability for success down the road.

Example: A manufacturing company and a software company will have to deal with two very different cost structures. While the software company can sell an additional unit at in theory no cost, the manufacturing company has a set of costs associated with each additional unit produced.

* * *

DOING YOUR HOMEWORK - PART II:
UNDERSTAND THE DEAL TERMS

"Price is what you pay. Value is what you get."

– WARREN BUFFET

What if I told you that you could invest in Uber back in 2009 when it was first founded? You knew that the business was a surefire success and bound to grow from where it was on that day. Would you want to invest? What if I told you that the only way you could invest in it was at a valuation (company value) of $1 trillion? Would you still want to invest?

The first three phases of our due diligence allow us to understand a deeper picture of the overall business and whether or not we could see it as successful down the road.

Someone once told me that "a great business does not necessarily make a great investment opportunity". It took me a minute to fully understand what this meant. How could a great business not make a great investment opportunity? If given the opportunity to invest in a company like Uber or AirBnb today, why wouldn't you take the chance? (assuming you believe they will grow from today)

What he was getting at is the fact that it is not just a good business that leads to a good investment opportunity. Instead, it is a good business paired with a good value that actually leads to a good investment opportunity. In the end, the quality of an investment depends on how much return you can get for buying into a company early on. As a result, it is critical that you understand the price that you are buying into the company at, or its valuation. (*Valuation: an estimation of a company's worth*)

The past three parts of your due diligence process prove critical to being able to understand whether or not you believe a business will be successful. However, especially in the case for equity crowdfunding, it is important to understand exactly what kind of value you are getting when buying a piece of a company.

THE ART OF COMPANY VALUATION

By understanding the valuation of the company, who performed it, and what metrics they used to determine it, you are best able to understand the value you will be getting on your investment.

Since the value that you as an investor receive from investing in a company through equity crowdfunding is directly tied to the value that is placed on the company, it is important to understand the sources of the final company valuation. Whether it was the company themselves who named their price, it was the platform who determined the valuation, or a past private round valuation was used, each poses a unique for the investor.

VALUATIONS DETERMINED BY A PLATFORM:

It is important to understand the incentives behind a platform themselves performing a valuation of a company. These platforms not only want to ensure that investors keep coming back over and over again but also that they are generating a strong reputation and pushing as much money as possible through their system in fair deals.

USING A PAST VALUATION:

Often times companies that go out for equity crowdfunding rounds have had previous investment rounds in the past. This past valuation can be important to understand as an investor coming in on a new round in order to understand how previous investors valued the business.

COMPANY DETERMINED VALUATIONS:

Obviously if the company is behind a valuation they are going to want to give themselves a far larger check than the public might value them at. Giving them more of a "bang for their buck" and losing less equity, this company is able to benefit at the loss of the end investor in order to raise additional funds.

OTHER METHODS OF VALUATION: INVESTING WITH A SYNDICATE

An alternative method of investing that you can take is by investing in a syndicate. Investing in a syndicate is similar to investing with a "crowd" of individuals except there is a greater level of control as to who can participate in the investment. Often times investments made through a syndicate will have a "lead investor" who can take charge of the investing process and negotiate the investment terms for the rest of the syndicate. By having a "lead investor" take control of the valuation that you are able to buy into, you as an investor are ensuring that you have a stronger voice in the investment and that your best interests are being accounted for.

UNDERSTANDING THE PAST AND PRESENT (FINANCES)

Away from understanding the price point that you would be buying into a company at, it is important to understand exactly where the company is projecting its finances moving forward. Often a critical part of any valuation, the ability to understand the financial health of a prospective investment opportunity will allow you as an investor to better gauge whether or not you believe the company will be successful down the road.

A couple key metrics to look in order to help evaluate the overall financial and business health of your prospective investment are:

- Revenue
- Gross Margin
- Burn Rate
- Customer Acquisition Cost
- Total User Base
- Total Active Users
- Total Engagement Metrics

Revenue: This is a key metric for many investors to look at as is able to show you the top line growth in a company. It gives you a quick snap shop as to how much money the company is able to generate as well as a closer look into revenue growth can show tremendous insights in how the company has been able to effectively scale. Month on month revenue can able be a helpful metric to look at as it isolates a company's revenue growth by month.

Gross Margin: This is a company's revenue minus is cost of goods sold. It gives you a better sense for exactly how profitable a company can be by understanding how much of its revenue goes to cover fixed costs.

Burn Rate: This is how much money a company is using on

a month to month basis. It can be helpful to understand as it shows us how much money the company needs to "keep the lights on" an overly high burn rate can be a red flag for investors as the company could be misusing the cash that they have. Similarly, it allows us to understand how long the company can operate with the money it currently has.

Customer Acquisition Cost (CAC): As its name suggests this is the cost for the company to acquire an additional customer. It is a helpful gauge to look at in order to understand how easily and efficiently a company will be able to scale as a lower CAC will mean less of a cost burden for the company to launch expansion efforts.

Total User Base: This is the total users that the business currently has. While not an accurate depiction of the overall profitability of the company, it is still an interesting statistic to look at in terms of better understanding the scale that a company has been able to reach.

Total Active Users: A more helpful gauge of a company's success with users is the total active users. This number, unlike its total user base, only accounts for individuals that are more frequently using the platform. As such it serves as a good gauge of growth for a company as you can easily track the growth of active users over time.

Engagement Metrics: These metrics track the less tangible aspects of the business. As such they should not be used to directly influence the value of a company, but merely to better understand the company's overall success.

UNDERSTANDING YOUR INVESTMENT TERMS

On top of understanding the valuation that you are buying into an investment at, it is important to fully understand the type of investment that you are making in a company. There are several key types of investments that you as an investor can enter into and as such it is important to understand the ins and outs of each.

The most common investment types are:

- Common Equity
- Preferred Equity
- Convertible Note
- SAFE (Developed by Y Combinator)

Common stock: These are the most traditional shares issued by a company. Often held by the founders and employees, Common shares typically hold voting rights but often less rights than are granted to Preferred shareholders. Common stockholders have the last claim to a company's assets after claims by debt holders and Preferred equity holders are met.

Preferred Equity: These are typically issued to outside investors. They have rights and conditions that are separate from those of your common stock holders. On a company-by-company basis, Preferred equity holders may have strategic measures in place to minimize the effects of dilution and control or influence the terms under which a company may be sold.

Convertible Note: These are widely used forms of investment in early stage companies. They are unsecured loans that converts to stock at some point in the future. Convertible Notes are useful in that they allow the investor to not set a fixed valuation on the company today, but instead incentivizes investors by rewarding them for investing at an early stage in the company. Using a valuation cap, discount rate, and an interest rate the value of your loan will appreciate over time, converting to equity come the next qualified round of financing.

SAFE (Simple Agreement for Future Equity): This is a unique instrument first developed by Y Combinator in 2013. It is similar to a convertible note in that is allows an investor to purchase equity at a future date. Unlike a convertible note, a SAFE is not a loan and does not accrue interest over time or have a maturity date. It similarly includes a variety of processes that simplify the overall investment.

Platform Specific Securities: As the equity crowdfunding industry has developed over time a variety of platforms have developed their own securities to streamline the investment process for the average investor. Just as we saw with the SAFE by Y Combinator, individual platforms are helping to streamline the process for investors by building their own investments types.

Now armed with a greater understanding of exactly where your company's valuation is coming from and the terms that you are agreeing to with a deal, it is important that you as an investor understand some events that could impact the value of your investment moving forward.

Valuation Shifting Events:

- Company Progress
- Company Challenges
- Market Dynamics
- A new priced equity round, acquisition, or IPO

By understanding what events can and will effect the value of your investment down the road you as investor can best prepare for long term success in all of your investments.

* * *

BUILDING AND GROWING YOUR INVESTMENT PORTFOLIO

Congratulations!

You have now gone through the hard work of finding and vetting your next great investment opportunity. You are far on your way to becoming a startup investor and reaping the many rewards that investing in early stage companies can have in the long run. Now they you have done the tough part of finding which company you want to invest in, it is time to put your money where your mouth is and add it to your portfolio.

But how much should you invest and how much are you able to actually invest through equity crowdfunding?

HOW MUCH CAN YOU INVEST?

Fortunately for us recent additions to the JOBS Act have allowed the everyday investor to participate in equity crowd-funding. With the minimum investment on some platforms starting as low as $100 you can invest in companies with incredibly small amounts.

However, you are similarly restricted with how much you are able to invest. Under new crowdfunding regulation entry level investors with a net income or net worth of less than $100,000 are able to invest either $2,000 or 5% of their annual income, whichever is greater. Similarly, if your net worth annual income are greater than $100,000 you are able to invest either 10% of your annual income or net work, whichever is less.

HOW MUCH SHOULD YOU INVEST?

As we touched upon earlier, you should understand your overall investment strategy before you invest in any given startup. By understanding exactly how much money you want to invest in early stage companies you are better able to understand exactly how much you should be putting behind a single startup investment. If you are looking to invest across a dozen or more businesses for instance you want to make sure that no investment is more than 10% of your overall startup investment funds. I recommend building a portfolio of no less than 10 to 15 stocks to make sure that your risk is more evenly spread across a variety of different investment opportunities.

So now that you made your first investment it is time to start building up your new startup portfolio for your own personal "venture capital fund".

BUILDING YOUR STARTUP PORTFOLIO

As mentioned before I think it's critical to have no less than 10 to 15 stocks in your portfolio. This does not need to happen immediately as I do not recommend you jump straight into ten different investment opportunities. Rather it is good to keep in mind how much money you want to invest overall and as opportunities present themselves to make sure that you are diversifying your investments into new and interesting startup opportunities.

∗ ∗ ∗

MANAGING YOUR STARTUP PORTFOLIO

Congratulations! You now have not only invested in a single startup, but have proven to be able to build a dynamic and strong portfolio of several startups to decrease your overall investment risk. Now comes the waiting game. As we mentioned the timeline for start up returns is typically 5-7 years, far longer than your typical public stock investment.

Unlike the stock market you as an investor are not provided with an update on the price of your investment on a day to day basis. Instead, it is important for you to monitor the success of the companies in your portfolio, understanding the trends and events that are critical for them over time.

Fortunately for you, many of the methods of investing in these startups require them to provide you as an investor with regular updates. As frequently as several times a year your portfolio company should provide you with a good update on how its business is doing.

A strong investment update should include not only the progress of the company, but any information about developments in the industry, potential business challenges, and ways in which you as an investor can help them grow the business. Occasionally these updates may even include requests for strategic advice or introductions from investors such as yourself. This is where the opportunity to invest in a startup can prove to be a truly unique experience for you as an investor as compare to investing in a public company.

IMPACTING YOUR INVESTMENT

What is unique about becoming it investor in an early stage company is that you as an individual can leverage your expertise to help personally grow your investment. What this means is that you can have a direct impact on this excess of the company that you are invested in, helping not only the company's long term success, but also directly pushing forward the investment you have placed in the company. This is where you can start to play the role of the role the typical venture capitalist in helping their portfolio companies move along and strategically grow over time.

THE TWO TYPES OF INVESTORS: ACTIVE VS. PASSIVE
THE ACTIVE INVESTOR:

An active investor would be one that we are describing above.

These individuals would be investors who could maintain a frequent dialogue with a portfolio company and do anything that they can to help provide strategic advice or other resources to grow the company over time.

THE PASSIVE INVESTOR:

Counter to an active investor's actions, a passive investor would be one who is more comfortable sitting back and letting their investment grow naturally over time. The nature of equity crowdfunding is that you as an investor often do not have the majority have a major stake in the company so your view may be that it is s not your worth your time to put the effort in to help actively grow the company. Instead, you as a passive investor may lean on others to help push the business forward.

In the end, the unique ability for you to take an active role in your investment proves to be a one the most interesting opportunities for equity crowdfunding. As a business can get access to thousands of unique and invested individuals with this business's best interest in mind you can together help push forward that not only the business, but the investors themselves.

HOW TO MAKE A PROFIT

Understanding exactly where your money is going and how

you hope to receive it back in the future is critical for you as an investor to understand. There are multiple outcomes that you could run into as a startup investor and it is important to understand each.

As an investor you could:

- Lose all of your Investment (The company goes bankrupt or shuts down)
- Recover some of your investment but not all of it
- Recover all of your original investment
- Return your original investment plus a small profit
- Earn a significant (5-10+ times) return on your investment

The goal is obviously for you as an investor to experience that 5th option with every company that you invest in. It is what we can only dream of with the opportunity to invest early in the next great company and have our investment grow far greater than we could have possibly imagined, resulting in a financial payday for the ages.

While you may have ten investments successful start of investors do not need a home run on every single one of their investments. Rather they need to make sure that overall their portfolio ends up with a positive return. As a result, you can have several companies go completely bankrupt and not return you any money, so long as you have a couple more that are able to return you some if not all of your original investment, a few more with a small multiple (2-3 times return) and just a single investment that returns a potentially 10+ times return. This is called the "power law", in which a few companies will generate the majority of the return for a fund.

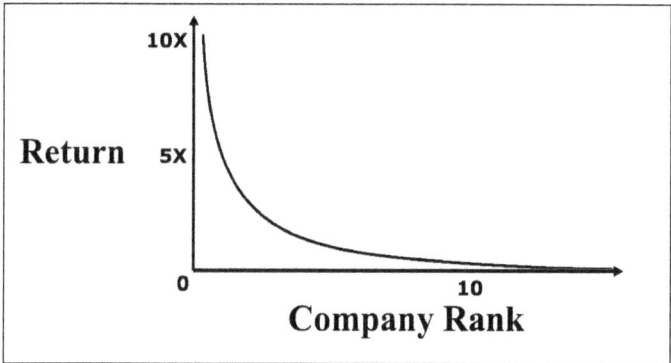

We as investors (with our own personal "VC Funds") should understand that this is how the typical real-world venture capital firm earns their returns and should not be greatly worried if we see one or two of our original investment start to take a downward dive.

RETURN ON INVESTMENT

Similarly, it is important to understand additional factors after your investment that can affect your position as an investor in the company.

Dilution: This is the reduction in your ownership percentage in a company due to them issuing additional newly created shares to new investors.

Follow on rounds: Most startups will raise multiple rounds of investment. Depending on the terms of your original investment you may be able to invest in thee future round and can allow you to further invest in the company.

Losses: As startup investing is so risky and a large number of investments will result in total or near loss of your original investment, it is important to monitor the companies in which you are invested.

Exits: These events are the ultimate goal of all startup investors. While so many startups fail to ever reach this stage of life, an exit means that you as an investor will receive your investment back and hopefully with a strong return attached to it. Whether through a liquidity event, an IPO, an acquisition, a secondary sale, or a recapitalization, these events will allow you to sell your stake in the company.

In the end, it is important to make sure that you are maximizing your return on investment when you make these risky startup investments. It can be valuable to closely monitor the progress of the companies over time to see if there are any opportunities to ask value from your side and play a more active role in your investments. Equity crowdfunding is a fascinating and unique opportunity in that it allows you as the investor an opportunity that is often reserved for the venture capitalists of the world, the ability to have a direct impact on your investments

* * *

RISKS

As with any investment it is important to fully understand the risks that come with your investment before you put your money behind it.

This could not hold more true with startup investing through equity crowdfunding as you are investing in some of the riskiest assets that you could be exposed to as an investor. However, with this risk comes the ability to earn returns that far outweigh nearly anything out there today thus still proving to be an attractive opportunity for many investors.

There are three key categories of risk that you should under-stand before you invest in equity crowdfunding. They are: 1) investment risks, 2) security risks, and 3) business risks. Each addressing unique part of your investment in a startup com-pany and should be understood before you invest any money.

INVESTMENT RISKS

Principle risk: You need to understand that when you make an investment in a startup you are putting that entire amount of money at risk. In no way are you obligated to see any of that original investment amount back if the company goes bankrupt. As such, you need to understand that the entire amount of money you originally invested could be lost if things go south for your company.

Returns risk: Similarly, it holds true that there's no guarantee on the returns. You're going to receive from a startup of investment. The returns through equity crowdfunding are highly variable and there is no way to predict exactly what sort of return you are going to receive in any amount or when you as an investor would receive a return on your investment

Returns delay: Unlike a publicly traded company that can be bought and sold almost instantly every day, early stage companies have a far longer timeline for investment (typically 5 to 7 years). It is important to understand this longer than normal horizon and the potential for additional delays before you would receive a return.

Liquidity risk: With this investment longer horizon, as of now it is difficult to sell your stake in any company. While over time we may see secondary markets develop, it as it currently stands no secondary market for private shares of early stage companies exists, making the ability to openly sell your ownership in a company difficult to nearly impossible.

SECURITY RISKS

Dilution: As investors we need to understand that the startup we put our money behind is likely going to raise additional money in the future. When additional investors enter the picture the company is likely to issue new securities and as such dilute your percentage of overall ownership in the company.

Valuation risk: Unlike their publicly traded counterparts with constant market driven prices, the valuation behind these private companies are far more difficult to determine. As such the pricing for a company can vary greatly depending on who you ask. it is important to understand that you risk potentially overpaying for your investment based on the valuation you enter into.

Business risks: There are a variety of different risks you need to understand when entering into an investment in an early stage company. Between revenue risks, funding risks, personnel risks, fraud, growth risk, and competition risk you need to understand that there is nothing set in stone as to how the company will perform or how the business environment around it will shape over time. As such you need to be fully aware that the environment and the situation the business operates in can shift at any point in time regardless of your investment.

∗ ∗ ∗

INVESTING IN FUNDS & AUTOMATING YOUR INVESTMENT

If the entire process of performing due diligence on companies and sifting through the available opportunities on a platform seems like too much for you as an investor, there is always the opportunity to automate your investments. As these equity crowdfunding marketplaces develop over time we are seeing more platforms give investors the opportunity to automate their selection of specific investments. Whether investing in a custom investment portfolio driven by the platforms themselves or investing through an investment club, there are a variety of different options to invest alongside or with people that you think could provide valuable opportunities down the road.

BENEFITS OF INVESTING WITH A FUND OR SYNDICATE

- Deal Flow
- Due Diligence
- Domain Knowledge

The benefit of doing this is that you still expose yourself to the benefits that can be had through early stage start investments, while streamlining the process on your side as an investor. By not dealing with the often time-consuming process that proper due diligence can be you are allowing yourself to invest part of your portfolio in early stage companies, without a large investment of time.

Whether you want to invest around a theme such as Y-Combinator startups or alongside investors that you think will be able to properly vet companies, more and more of these platforms are allowing you to more easily invest in these in early stage opportunities.

In the end, it is up to you how you want to navigate the dynamic and ever changing world of equity crowdfunding. The ability for the everyday investor to experience the risks and rewards of venture capital I believe will change our global entrepreneurial landscape. The ability for the next great wave of innovators and entrepreneurs to receive capital and support from their peers will reshape how our economy operates and launch us into an entirely new wave of economic opportunities.

SIX

THE NEW ECONOMY

———

"Crowdfunding will become the future of how small businesses are going to be financed."

- DUNCAN NEIDERAUER, FORMER CEO,
NEW YORK STOCK EXCHANGE

The emergence of this next generation of investing platforms and financial products is going to fundamentally reshape how individuals interact with their investments and profoundly change the world of finance. With millennials placing so much priority on understanding exactly where our money goes, it is important that we not only find a solution for our money to work smarter for us, but for it to work harder for us as well.

As we have seen, innovative solutions such as peer-to-peer

lending and equity crowdfunding offer investors the opportunity to get in on the ground floor of a new investing movement. It is an economic shift that is beginning to reshape the balance of power in the financial community and transform the process for how those who need capital receive it.

As the crowd-based capital raising movement expands, the next great wave of investors will discover new investment solutions and marketplace platforms being created on a day-to-day basis. These innovative solutions will provide a new staple for investing moving forward.

What is amazing about opportunities to invest in peer-to-peer lending and equity crowdfunding is not only the ability to generate a strong return of your investment, but also provides you to have a direct opportunity to create value in our economy. By this, I mean that your dollar given to a loan or a business has a direct ripple effect into how someone's is able to afford their mortgage or grow their business to the next level.

The more that we get people in the crowd investing economy, the more the next generation of those who are seeking funding can receive it from their peers. By directly supporting one another with capital, we as an ecosystem will ensure that we are generating an economic resurgence from the inside out, building value at our core and helping reshape our communities for the better.

LONG TERM SOCIAL BENEFITS

The opportunity to secure investments from the crowd and to directly invest into those individuals and businesses who need it most will lead to a fundamental reshaping of how we are able to contribute to our greater community.

DOWNSIDE OF INVESTING IN THE STOCK MARKET:

It is hard for you, as an investor, to understand exactly where your dollar is going in the stock market. The reality is that when you invest in the stock market you are simply placing a bet. You are betting that your investment will rise in value. Your money goes to the person from whom you have purchased the stock. The company receives nothing. So you have really not contributed to the company in any way. You are in no way directly helping the company. It's a bet, plain and simple. When push comes to shove, where really is your value being created? If you had the opportunity to invest that dollar directly to someone else or another small business for the same return would you do it?

* * *

As the sharing economy continues to reach deeper into the traditional economy, we as millennial's are looking for more ways that we can add value through how we invest. The world of alternative finance will encourage a movement of individuals looking for their money to not only work smarter for them but work harder for them. We are going to be able to support those around us and allow those who may have not been able to seek a loan from a bank, to get support from their neighbors and peers all of whom will benefit in the end.

The economic surge that will result from this movement is going to be monumental and provide a tremendous boost to our overall economy. By taking money out of the more static capital markets and putting it directly at work with those who need it, we as a community can help foster economic development from the inside out, helping to support small businesses and individuals.

No longer will we need to go through the massive banks to get funding for the next business expansion or loan, but instead we can rely on our own peers who not only can show faith in us, but realize and financial benefit in the long term as well.

This concept of "crowd-based capital raising" is going to reshape how we are able to leverage our networks for the positive benefit of our community at large. As we have seen time and time again, social networks possess a tremendous amount of power to transform society. By coming together as a community of investors to support our peers and support value creation for an emerging business, we will be able to impact the lives of both the borrower and the lender, reaping tremendous success down the road.

DIRECT IMPACT ON ECONOMIC GROWTH

"A man's true wealth is the good he has done to his fellow man"

- MAHATMA GANDHI

By investing directing into the people and businesses around us, we as a community will have a direct impact on the economic growth of our communities and our greater economy at large. At no other time in history have you been able to so directly impact the financial economy and the economy around you. I believe that we will see a fundamental rebirth of American economic success. As a nation of small businesses and entrepreneurs we have long relied upon our great innovators and small business owners to create lasting value in our communities. However, as the banks became "too big to fail" we began to see more and more of the economic potential of our nation being locked up by a small number of very large and powerful organizations. By allowing individuals to invest money away from the stock market and directly into the heart of our economy, all Americans can now play direct and immediate role in helping to advance our economy, driving the next great wave of value creation.

Down the road, I believe investors will look to not only the financial return that they receive from their investment, but the impact and value creation that their invested dollars will have in the end. If you can receive the same return helping to support "Sally's" loan who would not have been able to get it through a bank or merely put it in the market, I am certain that more often than not people are going to support their peers.

* * *

YOUR PLAYBOOK FOR GETTING STARTED

Let's take a look at how you as an investor can get started investing in the fascinating world of alternative finance.

To get a better gauge on how you as an investor can get started with these emerging platforms, we will break down three unique pathways, accounting for the various factors that separate investors.

FACTORS TO UNDERSTAND BEFORE INVESTING:

- Investor Status: Are an accredited or unaccredited investor?
- Available Money: How much are you able to invest?
- Risk Tolerance: How much risk you are willing to take with your investments?

By understanding these three factors as well as various others, we are able to craft a tailored blueprint as to you should approach your overall investment strategy. Along with this tailored blueprint we will take a look at the various investment options available to you and where they can sit in to your overall portfolio.

INVESTMENT OPTIONS TO UNDERSTAND:

- Managed wealth management accounts such as Betterment & Wealthfront
- Free to trade investing through Robinhood
- Peer to Peer Investments (Automated & Manual)
- Equity Crowdfunding (As an Individual & with a syndicate)
- AngelList Syndicates (Accredited)

THE NEED FOR A BALANCED PORTFOLIO

Just as it is crucial for you to have a diversified portfolio of loans or companies in your peer to peer and equity crowdfunding portfolios, it is important that your overall portfolio be spread across various investment types.

THE 70-30 MODEL

Historically investors have looked to the "70-30" allocation model to keep their portfolios in check. This model, referencing a 70% investment in stocks, compared to a 30% investment in bonds, looks to help investors experience the positive upward growth of bull markets in stocks while minimizing the shock of down market conditions through a stable bond

THE NEW ECONOMY · 163

options available to you and where they can sit in to your overall portfolio.

(fixed-income) position. As investors look to expose themselves to different risk in alternative investments, many will lower their stocks and bond holdings to invest in alternatives (sometimes investing upwards of 15% of their portfolio).

As we look to understanding how to best balance our investment strategy using alternative methods such as peer to peer lending and equity crowdfunding, it is important that we learn from investors who have already seen success in these assets.

MEET THE YALE ENDOWMENT

Unlike the 70-30 portfolio mentioned above, Yale's endowment using a strategy all their own. While the typical investor may put upwards of 15-20% in alternative investment types, Yale's invests almost 50% of its endowment in them.

"The Endowment's long time horizon is well suited to exploiting illiquid, less efficient markets such as venture capital, leveraged buyouts, oil and gas, timber, and real estate."

- YALE ON THEIR ENDOWMENT

Take venture capital for instance. Today, Yale's endowment invests over 16% of its portfolio into venture capital. How has its success been over the last decade? For Yale, its venture capital investments have returned an average of 18% per year.

As a result, Yale's endowment continues its deep alternative investments with 14% in real estate and nearly 7% in natural resources (timber, etc.).

While we as investors may not seek to mimic the 50% allocation to alternatives that Yale uses, your holding in alternatives could span anywhere from 10% to 25% of your portfolio depending on the risk you are willing to take. As investors, it is important to understand how Yale has experienced success with these investments in the past and how their positions compare with traditional stock and bond holdings.

* * *

In the end, the following three tracks should leave you with a tangible set of guidelines as to how to move forward and enter into the fascinating and rapidly growing worth of alternative finance.

TRACK #1: YOU ARE AN UNACCREDITED INVESTOR WITH $5,000 TO INVEST AND LITTLE MONEY CURRENTLY IN THE STOCK MARKET.

As you are new to the investing world and peer to peer lending and equity crowdfunding prove risky in their own ways, it is important that you as an investor balance your investment strategy with a stable portfolio of stocks and bonds. By beginning your investment strategy on stable ground with a diversified portfolio in the public markets you will best ensure your financial health over time.

Of your $5,000 to invest we recommend that you invest between $3,000 and $3,500 in a Betterment or WealthFront account (60-70% of your portfolio). These platforms will allow you to easily tailor your investment strategy based on your risk tolerance and have the system automatically manage your investment account for you. As a new investor, you may also want to take $500 or so from this chunk of your portfolio and place it in a Robinhood investing account. Through their innovative and free-to-trade platform you will be able to have a more active presence over your investments, even making trades on the go.

We recommend taking the remaining money that you have to invest and splitting your investments between peer to peer lending and equity crowdfunding (approximately 70% of the remaining funds invested in peer to peer compared to 30% in equity crowdfunding). The balance between these two is all relative to the risk you are willing to take as an investor. We recommend that at the beginning you take a more conservative route, leaning on peer to peer loans for more stable returns. Assuming that you placed $3000 in your wealth management account your portfolio would look like this:

- Wealthfront / Betterment: $3000
- Peer to Peer Lending: $1400
- Equity Crowdfunding: $600

For your $1,400 peer to peer investment portfolio, you can look to either manual filter through loans or leverage automated investments. By using an automated investment account, you can earn the benefits that come with peer to peer investing while maintaining a more hand-off approach.

With the remaining $600 you should look to make the most out of the exciting world of equity crowdfunding. With many platforms having minimum investment sizes of $100 it will be tough to gather a fully diversified portfolio with only $600. Instead, I recommend turning to funds such as WeFunder's Orange Funds, which will allow you to tap into a more diversified and complete portfolio of startups with a smaller investment.

If you do decide to go out and invest in your own choices of high growth companies, we recommend that you perform a deep level of due diligence as your risk will be far greater than under a more comprehensive portfolio of 15-20 investments. In the end, as an unaccredited investor, it is important to leverage the best platform out there to ensure that your money is being put to work in the best way possible.

TRACK #2: YOU ARE AN ACCREDITED INVESTOR WHO ALREADY HAS MONEY INVESTED IN THE STOCK MARKET, BUT IS LOOKING TO INVEST $10,000 IN ALTERNATIVES.

As of today you as an accredited investor have a leg up on your unaccredited counterparts. A key part of investing in equity crowdfunding is the quality of deals (deal flow) that you are exposed to. We are still seeing many of the top quality deals on platforms that remain exclusively for accredited investors. You as an accredited investor can leverage platforms such as AngelList to invest alongside some of the top angel investors and syndicates across the world.

As a savvy investor with an existing stock and bond portfolio, we recommend you take a more aggressive approach to your investment strategy. Unlike building a balanced investment portfolio from the ground up, we recommend that you take a 50-50 or more balance between your peer to peer and equity investments. Depending on the risk level you are comfortable with we even recommend investing as much as 65-70% of your alternative portfolio into equity crowdfunding ($6,500 - $7,000). As you are able to build out a comprehensive portfolio of investments, we recommend you gain exposure to the tremendous upsides that can be offered through early stage investments.

To begin your investments, we recommend that you find the

best syndicates out there and commit to writing checks as small as a $1,000 to each investment they enter into. By going out and finding interesting investors that you want to pair your investments with, you not only get access to tremendous deal flow and investment opportunities, but you are able to leverage their due diligence and source some of the most exclusive deals available on the marketplace.

We have seen a variety of funds launch who are able to leverage this sort of tactic to streamline the due diligence process on their end and lever the knowledge and experience of previously successful investors.

TRACK #3: YOU ARE AN UNACCREDITED INVESTOR LOOKING TO GET STARTED WITH ALTERNATIVES AND INVEST $10,000.

We recommend that you begin your alternative investing portfolio with a balanced 60-40 peer-to-peer lending and equity crowdfunding positions ($6,000 peer to peer and $4,000 towards equity investments). This more balanced approach allows you to have a strong peer to peer base that can generate returns over time while similarly entering into a riskier equity investment portfolio. As the investor, you should feel comfortable adjusting your portfolio given your risk comfort, but overall you should understand the importance of having healthy diversification.

With your $6,000 peer to peer investment, we recommend placing it in an automated investment account so as to ease the burden on your end and allow for your investment to best align with your overall risk preferences.

We recommend that you begin your $4,000 equity allocation by writing small checks across a variety of different investment opportunities. Whether you want to take a hands-on approach and write small $100 checks across twenty-five different companies or look to invest alongside some of the smartest investors through a fund, you should look to begin to build a diversified portfolio over time.

As an unaccredited investor, it is important that you understand the platforms on which you are making your investments. Often the quality of the deals available are directly related to the quality of the platform. As such, you should do your research on the platforms before committing to any one.

* * *

All in all, it is important to understand that equity crowdfunding is a riskier investment than peer to peer lending. Investors should look to invest no more than they are willing to lose it into early stage companies.

We recommend a strategy that investors balance their

alternative investment portfolios with a diversified stocks and bonds position. We have seen many investors successfully utilize a similar strategy to the one mentioned in Track #1 in which a portfolio contains 65% public stocks and bonds and the remaining 35% is split between peer to peer lending, equity crowdfunding, and other alternative investment strategies. In the end, how you want to allocate your portfolio is directly connected to the risk that you are willing to take and the quality of deals you are afforded.

Whether you want to invest $5,000 or $500,000, the same principles listed above can easily be adjusted regardless of how much you are investing.

* * *

There is a massive sharing movement at birth that is about to reshape our economy. As we can rely upon the crowd to benefit overall, the world of investing will not only be reshaped by technology but will allow individuals to reap a greater direct social benefit from investing in those around them.

The next generation of investors are going to have a direct influence on the growth of the economy around them and be able to support the people who are most at need for financing. In the end, peer-to-peer lending and equity crowdfunding open the floodgates for a wave of value creation. In our sharing economy where we rely so much upon others, the world of crowd investing is allowing us to take our "blind" money in the stock markets and actively put it to work through those around us, spurring growth from the ground up and launching the next great wave of innovation.

SEVEN

FINANCE 2.0: THE NEXT WAVE OF INVESTING

"Without change there is no innovation, creativity, or incentive for improvement. Those who initiate change will have a better opportunity to manage the change that is inevitable."

– WILLIAM POLLARD

The emergence of alternative finance and the various types of new investment opportunities that are presented investors through peer-to-peer lending and equity crowdfunding will reshape how individuals approach the overall world of investments.

As millennials, we greatly value the ability to have more of a direct influence and understanding as to where our hard earned money is being put to work. Far too often individuals are turned off by the intricacies of understanding the stock market. In fact, a majority of millennials say that the main reason that they do not invest in the stock market, away from not having enough money, is that it is too complex to understand.

As technology has changed with the times and made various parts of our lives easier to use, the stock market has stayed behind, still making it ever more difficult for the next generation to learn how to invest in it.

The emergence of peer-to-peer lending and equity crowdfunding and their unique digital approach to investing make it easier than ever for individuals to understand where they are putting their money and exactly how the money is getting put to work.

The FinTech revolution is reshaping finance from the ground up. Its effort to reshape alternative finance is going to change not only peer-to-peer lending and equity crowdfunding but have a far greater reach down the road. The next great wave of investing will mean that individuals no longer solely invest in the public stock market, but instead expand their reach to more intricate and interesting digitally accessible options.

As peer-to-peer lending allows for individuals to invest in loans and equity crowdfunding allows individuals to invest direct into high growth businesses we are at the forefront of this massive technological shift in investing. I believe that we are only cracking the surface in how we can bring the old world of investing into the digital age.

In the future the next tech savvy investor won't merely be limited to investing in a loan or equity through peer-to-peer lending or equity crowdfunding. Instead what we will see is a resurgence of a variety of unique investment opportunities that today have been closed off to only the wealthiest institutional investors out there.

What we will see is the democratization of the massive world of direct alternative investments. By taking these entities that were once closed off to the everyday man and opening it up and allowing them to invest, we will allow them to invest in unique opportunities they had previously never been able to.

Some of the unique investment opportunities that I believe will open up for the crowd to invest in are:

- Real Estate (We are already seeing tremendous success)
- Infrastructure
- Agriculture
- Mining

- Timber
- Solar
- Industrials
- Telecommunications

While we as investors today may not be able to invest directly into a mine in Colorado or solar panel in Argentina, the democratization of investing and the movement of crowd investing will reshape the future of a millennial's investment opportunities. In the end we will allow our dollars to work not only harder, but smarter for us as we are able to leverage technology to find opportunities to invest that we never could have found before.

We are already seeing the start of this movement.

Meet SunFunder. SunFunder is an innovative platform that is at the forefront of the next generation of alternative finance investment types. SunFunder is a solar finance business based in San Francisco with a mission to unlock capital for solar energy in the emerging world. It's model, through using the crowd, aggregates capital through a unique fund and offers the opportunity for investors to invest in a diversified, vetted, and high impact portfolio of unique solar projects. SunFunder then takes this capital and deploys it in a unique way to help deploy solar systems and catalyze growth across the markets that they reach across the emerging markets that they are focused on.

Having already closed a fund over were worth over $15 million we are just at the start of solutions such as SunFunder. While typical banks in the past would have closed off the opportunity to make an investment in a rural and developing region, SunFunder is able to thrive because of their ability to lever the crowd and leverage investors who see the value in investing in diversifying their portfolio across unique investments opportunities that can provide a differentiated impact in the end.

Just as peer-to-peer lending and equity crowdfunding were able to lever the crowd investing money of so many to foster lasting change to those who needed it, innovative projects such as SunFunder will push this democratization of investing to new found heights. What we will see are companies pushing these limits and entering into unique types investments that the everyday investor never would have previously had access to. We are at the forefront of this movement, but in the future I believe that the typical investor place far more money than ever thought possible in innovative investment projects backed by the crowd.

CONCLUSION

———

What a time to be alive.

We are living in one of the greatest technological and entrepre-neurial revolutions our global economy has ever experienced and it's impacting every single aspect of our lives.

We have already seen the Uber's and Airbnb's of the world flip the transportation and hospitality industries on their heads. The emerging sharing economy is reaching far wider than we could possibly have ever imagined and it has already set its sights on one of the biggest industries of our time, finance.

As we have seen, the emergence of FinTech is ripping through the financial services industry and reshaping nearly every single aspect of how an individual deals with their day to day financial and investing decisions. The emergence of alternative finance solutions, such as peer-to-peer lending and equity crowdfunding, represent a fundamental shift in how the next generation and we as millennials will directly engage in new forms of investing and how in doing so we can shape our investment future.

These new investing platforms allow us to not only generate a positive return on our investment, but also to directly impact an economic resurgence in our communities from the ground up. By giving money to those who need it most, the peer-to-peer and equity crowdfunding movement represents part of a greater shift towards the individuals using technology and social networks to support one another.

This is the world of "crowd-based capital raising". Whether it is through peer-to-peer loans or raising money for a high growth startup through crowdfunding, this movement will fundamentally reshape our investing world. The emergence of the types of powerful technology-driven and socially-powered investing networks that we have begun to see today in peer-to-peer lending and equity crowdfunding are only scratching the surface of what this massive movement will deliver to the marketplace in the coming years.

While you as an investor may look to start with $5,000 to invest across these innovative platforms today, the scale of investment opportunities that we are about to witness across this industry will enable one to grow a portfolio from investing $5,000 to $500,000 far quicker than you might have imagined. As investors become accustomed to deploying capital through these networks, the number of platforms and scale of investment opportunities are sure to grow.

What we as investors need to understand is that, overall, the principle is the same whether you are investing $100 or $100,000. Just as the great investors of the past started building their skills by using the money from their paper routes to buy one or two shares of stock in a company they thought held promise as an investment, the savvy millennial needs to understand that the crowd-based capital raising movement is here to stay. It is time to understand how it is going to reshape our world and learn how to participate as an investor. Peer-to-peer lending and equity crowdfunding offer a fundamental change in how we as investors can positively benefit our community while allowing our money to not only work harder but smarter for us.

It is opening up a world of possibilities for individuals and companies who may have otherwise been turned down by the big banks and classic venture firms, allowing the crowd to voice their opinion and financially support the great next great ideas of tomorrow and in doing so help those who need it most.

Direct investing, whether peer-to-peer lending or equity crowdfunding enables an individual to engage directly in both their local community as well as other communities and markets of interest. How many of you have ever seen a business that you like and wish that you could help grow? With investment vehicles such as peer-to peer lending and equity crowdfunding you are given the opportunity to directly lend or invest in those businesses that would have in the past been completely closed off to you. This fundamental shift of how we as a community can support one another is going to lead to an economic surge that will create far greater value than we could possibly imagine.

We are just at the leading edge of the crowd-based movement and the opportunities for growth are truly endless. As the power of the crowd can make such a big impact, we as millennials need to understand the value that comes in investing with one another and the great opportunities of tomorrow.

Opportunities such as peer-to-peer lending and equity crowdfunding allow the crowd to collectively reap far greater benefits than any one individual could do alone.

It is going to will reshape how our economy operates and will become a pivotal part of our lives moving forward.

Now is the time for millennials to take note. These platforms are giving us a glimpse into the next generation of investing and it's here to stay.

WEBSITES TO VISIT

___

FIN-TECH

- Robinhood Investing: www.Robinhood.com
- Betterment: www.Betterment.com
- Wealthfront: www.Wealthfront.com

PEER-TO-PEER LENDING

- Lending Club: www.LendingClub.com
- Prosper: www.Prosper.com
- Funding Circle: www.FundingCircle.com
- NSR Invest: www.NSRInvest.com
- LendingRobot: www.LendingRobot.com
- BlueVestment: www.BlueVestment.com
- PeerCube: www.PeerCube.com

- Lend Academy: www.LendAcademy.com
- NSR Platform: www.NSRPlatform.com
- Lending Memo: www.LendingMemo.com
- Orchard: www.OrchardPlatform.com/Blog
- Lendit Conference: www.LendIt.com

EQUITY CROWDFUNDING

- AngelList: www.Angel.co/Invest
- WeFunder: www.WeFunder.com
- Fundable: www.Fundable.com
- CircleUp: www.CircleUp.com
- SeedInvest: www.SeedInvest.com
- Crowdfunder: www.Crowdfunder.com
- FundersClub: www.FundersClub.com
- OurCrowd: www.OurCrowd.com
- Seedrs: www.Seedrs.com
- FrontFundr: www.FrontFundr.com
- EquityNet: www.EquityNet.com
- LocalStake: www.LocalStake.com

REAL ESTATE CROWDFUNDING

- Peer Street: www.PeerStreet.com
- Real Crowd: www.RealCrowd.com
- Realty Mogul: www.RealtyMogul.com
- RealtyShares: www.RealtyShares.com

- Acquire Real Estate: www.AcquireRealEstate.com
- LendingHome: www.LendingHome.com
- Roofstock: www.RoofStock.com
- Patch of Land: www.PatchOfLand.com
- EarlyShares: www.EarlyShares.com
- CrowdStreet: www.CrowdStreet.com
- FundRise: www.FundRise.com
- Groundfloor: www.GroundFloor.us
- FundThatFlip: www.FundThatFlip.com
- iFunding: www.iFunding.co

ALTERNATIVE INVESTMENT PLATFORMS

- YieldStreet: www.YieldStreet.com
- SunFunder: www.SunFunder.com

REFERENCES

___

CHAPTER 1: INVESTING TODAY

- https://blog.crowdfunder.com/
  how-millennials-will-change-the-face-of-finance-investing/
- http://vintagevalueinvesting.com/how-to-invest-in-
  water-like-michael-burry-from-the-big-short/
- http://www.telegraph.co.uk/finance/personalfinance/
  investing/11519612/Beware-the-risks-before-invest-
  ing-in-the-booming-art-market.html
- http://money.usnews.com/investing/
  articles/2016-06-08/how-to-invest-in-wine
- http://www.rliland.com/the-basics-of-timberland-investing
- http://vintagevalueinvesting.com/how-to-invest-in-
  water-like-michael-burry-from-the-big-short/

- https://www.wilmingtontrust.com/repositories/wtc_site-content/PDF/Investing-Collectible-Cars-2015.pdf
- http://money.usnews.com/investing/articles/2016-02-17/how-to-invest-in-classic-cars

CHAPTER 2: A FINTECH REVOLUTION

- https://s3-us-west-2.amazonaws.com/nsr-invest/white-papers/The-Financial-Advisor%27s-Guide-to-P2Pi.pdf
- https://blog.crowdfunder.com/fintech-trends-wealth-management-and-the-rise-of-robo-advisors/
- http://venturebeat.com/2016/05/05/square-reports-379-million-in-revenue-for-q1-as-gross-payment-volume-spikes-45/
- https://twitter.com/RobinhoodApp/status/785985881291296768?lang=en
- https://www.google.com/finance?q=NYSE%3ALC&ei=EvJvWKlGiOGYAfL8mcgH

CHAPTER 3: THE NEW ECONOMY

- https://www.fundable.com/learn/resources/guides/crowdfunding-guide/what-is-crowdfunding
- https://www.a-connect.com/acknowledge/a-brief-history-of-the-sharing-economy-and-its-future-path/
- http://www.economist.com/news/leaders/21573104-internet-everything-hire-rise-sharing-economy
- http://www.sethgodin.com/sg/bio.asp

- http://www.azquotes.com/quotes/topics/kickstarter.html
- http://collider.com/simon-helberg-i-am-i-interview/
- https://techcrunch. com/2014/03/26/a-brief-history-of-oculus/
- http://www.eurogamer.net/articles/2013-07-11-happy-go-luckey-meet-the-20-year-old-creator-of-oculus-rift

CHAPTER 4: A PEER TO PEER REVOLUTION

- http://www.lendacademy.com/ p2p-lending-best-practices-2016-an-investors-guide/
- http://www.lendingmemo.com/ebook
- http://www.altfi.com/images/upload/arti-cleimages/ppvolume.png
- http://www.lendingmemo.com/ diversification-lending-club-prosper/
- https://dspace.mit.edu/bitstream/han-dle/1721.1/80161/43697786-MIT.pdf?sequence=2
- http://www.premierbusinesslending.com/alternative-lending/ how-alternative-lending-works-and-helps-economy/
- http://docs.nsrinvest.com/getting-started-with-peer-to-peer-lending/getting-started-guide/ why-is-p2p-lending-an-attractive-investment-opportunity
- http://thelendingmag.com/peer-to-peer-lending/#av1
- http://www.lendingmemo.com/ diversification-lending-club-prosper/

- http://www.lendacademy.com/
  diversification-and-p2p-lending-part-1/
- https://www.lendingrobot.com/#/
- https://techcrunch.com/2016/01/30/the-state-of-p2p-lending/
- https://www.nsrinvest.com/wp-uploads/www.nickel-
  steamroller.com/2016/03/NSR-Get-Started-8-14-15_2.pdf
- http://www.lendingmemo.com/ebook
- http://www.lendacademy.com/updated-super-sim-
  ple-filter-strategies-for-lending-club-and-prosper/
- http://www.lendingmemo.com/
  redlining-florida-lending-club-prosper/

CHAPTER 5: EQUITY CROWDFUNDING

- https://fundersclub.com/learn/guides/vc-101/
  the-risks-and-rewards-of-startup-investing/
- https://www.seedinvest.com/academy/
  startup-portfolio-planning
- http://earlyinvesting.com/
  more-equity-crowdfunding-success-stories/
- https://blog.crowdfunder.com/startup-investing-guide/
- https://microventures.com/
  building-investment-portfolio-startups
- https://microventures.com/equity-crowdfunding
- http://www.banklesstimes.com/2015/11/02/qa-with-ken-
  dall-almerico-on-title-iii-equity-crowdfunding-rules/
- http://www.foodrepublic.

com/2016/08/08/u-s-investors-are-pouring-money-into-scottish-craft-beer-darling-brewdog/

- http://www.techbullion.com/equity-crowdfunding-fintech-impacting-equity-crowdfunding/
- https://microventures.com/analyzing-startup-part-iii-value-proposition
- https://microventures.com/understanding-a-startups-financial-projections
- https://microventures.com/essential-vc-terms-know
- https://microventures.com/defining-microventures-late-stage-offerings
- https://microventures.com/evaluating-a-startup-these-7-metrics-can-help
- https://microventures.com/how-the-mv-investment-committee-selects-startups
- https://microventures.com/what-is-a-convertible-note
- https://microventures.com/evolution-equity-crowdfunding
- https://wefunder.com/faq/investors#expectations-and-risk
- http://tuckermax.me/how-crowdfunding-will-change-the-world-part-3-investing/

CHAPTER 6: THE NEW ECONOMY

- https://microventures.com/how-equity-crowdfunding-supports-local-restaurants
- https://www.seedinvest.com/blog/crowdfunding/crowdfunding-could-be-a-job-creator-and-a-6-2-billion-ma

- https://www.bloomberg.com/news/articles/2015-10-06/yale-endowment-model-thrives-as-swensen-proteges-post-top-gains
- http://www.financialsamurai.com/a-look-inside-investment-asset-allocation-of-massive-university-endowments/

CHAPTER 7: FINANCE 2.0: THE NEXT WAVE OF INVESTING

- https://www.youtube.com/watch?v=tjVGSeoUQk8
- https://www.crowdsurfer.com/blog/crowdfunding-green-energy-in-europe/
- https://www.crowdsurfer.com/blog/panel-discussion-the-disruptive-power-of-democratised-finance-and-how-it-changes-everything/
- https://www.crowdsurfer.com/blog/the-future-of-crowdfunding--with-crowdsurfer/
- https://www.crowdsurfer.com/blog/the-next-generation-of-crowd-finance-intelligence/
- https://www.crowdsurfer.com/blog/6-reasons-why-crowd-finance-is-here-to-stay/
- http://sunfunder.com/
- https://daraalbrightmedia.com/2016/08/11/can-micro-investing-technology-reverse-americas-harrowing-wealth-gap/
- https://daraalbrightmedia.com/2016/09/08/the-impact-of-micro-investing-technology-that-no-one-is-talking-about/

- https://daraalbrightmedia.com/wp-content/ uploads/2016/07/the-renaissance-of-the-retail-investor-white-paper-481611.pdf
- https://daraalbrightmedia.com/blog/page/2/